Preface

Within the framework of its programme of activities for the biennium 1988–1989, UNESCO asked a team of members of the International Council for Science Policy Studies (ICSPS) to carry out, under contract, a study on future trends in science and technology policies. ICSPS, which is a section of the International Union for the History and Philosophy of Science (IUHPS), itself a member of the International Council of Scientific Unions (ICSU), is an interdisciplinary association grouping together some eighty researchers of international standing who represent the main schools of thought in science policy studies worldwide.

The study prepared by ICSPS entitled 'Science, Technology and Developing Countries – Strategies for the 90s' analyses the present international context of which the new techno-industrial system is a feature and establishes a typological classification of developing countries according to their scientific and technological potential. The authors then propose, for each type of country, alternative development scenarios for the next ten years, and science and technology policies that would make it possible to take up the challenges of each scenario. The study ends with a series of recommendations and conclusions concerning the central role of science and technology in the process of development, the pre-conditions for the establishment and operation of a scientific and technological base, the management of available scientific and technological resources, new techno-industrial policies, and the value of international scientific and technological co-operation.

Although UNESCO does not necessarily share all the authors' points of view, it wishes this future-oriented study to be made known and widely distributed. The viewpoints expressed here are often new, sometimes provocative, but always stimulating. The lessons to be drawn from the study could offer new and helpful insights for developing countries and for the Organization in its work in those countries.

Science and technology in developing countries

Science and technology in developing countries

Strategies for the 1990s

UNESCO

The authors are responsible for the choice and the presentation
of the facts contained in this book and for the opinions expressed
therein, which are not necessarily those of UNESCO and do
not commit the Organization.

Published in 1992 by the United Nations Educational,
Scientific and Cultural Organization
7 place de Fontenoy, 75700 Paris
Typeset by UNESCO
Printed by Imprimerie de la Manutention, Mayenne
ISBN 92–3–102739–5
© UNESCO 1992
Printed in France

Contents

Acknowledgements

This report represents in many respects a synthesis of discussions held at meetings of the International Council for Science Policy Studies (ICSPS) on several occasions in recent years. It would be thus impossible to thank individually all those who have indirectly contributed, and who include members of the Council as well as non-members who participated in several sessions.

The working group has, however, also been able to draw upon a number of direct contributions from members of the Council. In particular, special thanks are due to Dr Li Poxi (China), Dr I. Malecki (Poland), Dr V. I. Maslennikov (USSR), Dr M. J. Moravcsik (United States), Dr F. Sagasti (Peru), Dr K. Singh (India) and Dr P. Tamas (Hungary), whose initial inputs played a decisive role in setting the orientation of the report.

In its present final version, the report has been completed, discussed and approved by a working group of the following: Dr S. Finquelievich (Argentina), Professor M. Gibbons (United Kingdom), Dr A. Grübler (International Institute for Applied Systems Analysis), Dr Papa Kane (Senegal), Professor-Dr G. Kröber (Germany), Professor H. Nowotny (Austria), Professor H. Rattner (Brazil), Professor J.-J. Salomon (France), Dr J. Sutz (Uruguay), and Dr Wang Hui Jiong (China). Brief biographical notes on the members of this working group will be found in the List of Authors below.

Although they are greatly indebted to all those who contributed to the preparation of this report, the members of the working group assume full responsibility for the final product.

List of authors

Dr Susana Finquelievich is an architect and holds a Ph.D. in urban sociology. She is currently Senior Researcher with the National Council for Scientific and Technical Research (CONICET) and the Center for Urban and Regional Studies (CEUR), both in Buenos Aires (Argentina), and Director of the CEUR-CONICET research project on Technological Innovation in Metropolitan Areas.

Professor Michael Gibbons is Professor of Science and Technology Policy, and Director of the Programme of Policy Research in Engineering Science and Technology (PREST) at the University of Manchester, United Kingdom. He has published widely in the field of science policy, the economics of technological change and the evolution of research. He has for many years been an advisor to national governments and various organizations in the public and private sectors.

Dr Arnulf Grübler is affiliated to the Technology, Economy and Society Programme of the International Institute for Applied Systems Analysis (IIASA), a non-governmental, international research institute located in Laxenburg, Austria. He holds a Ph.D. in regional development planning and science. His research focuses on the long-term dynamics of technical and economic change, with emphasis on energy and transport.

Dr Papa Kane, an economist from Senegal, is Director of the Centre Interafricain pour le Développement de la Formation Professionnelle, which is located in Abidjan (Côte d'Ivoire) and attached to the International Labour Organisation. His previous appointments include that of Professor, then Director, of the École Nationale d'Économie Appliquée (ENEA) in Senegal.

Professor-Dr Gunter Kröber holds a Ph.D. in mathematics and philosophy, and is was formerly Director of the Institute for Theory, History and Organization of Science of the Academy of Sciences of the German Democratic Republic. His main research fields are related to the history and philosophy of science, and to science and society.

Professor Helga Nowotny is Professor and Director of the Institute for Theory and Social Studies of Science at the University of Vienna, and Chairperson of the Standing Committee for the Social Sciences of the European Science Foundation. She holds a doctorate in law and a Ph.D. in sociology, and her research work is in the fields of social policy and social studies of science.

Professor Henrique Rattner holds a Ph.D. in economics, and is currently Professor of Economics at the University of São Paulo. He has been an adviser with a number of national and international organizations, and has published several books on science, technology and industrial policy.

Dr Jean-Jacques Salomon is Professor at the Conservatoire National des Arts et Métiers (CNAM) in Paris, and Director of its research centre Science Technologie et Société. His publications include *Science et politique, L'écrivain public et l'ordinateur,* and most recently *Science, guerre et paix.*

Dr Judith Sutz is an electrical engineer who holds a Ph.D. in development planning. She is currently Researcher at the Centro de Informaciones Estudios del Uruguay (CIESU), in Montevideo, and co-ordinates the project 'Uruguay: Problems and Prospects of the Electronic Industrial System in a Small Country'.

Wang Hui Jiong is Executive Director of the Development Research Centre of the State Council of the People's Republic of China. He has had forty years of working experience in engineering, S&T policy and macroeconomic policy studies. Major publications include: *China Toward the Year 2000* (in English) and *An Introduction to Systems Engineering* (in Chinese).

Introduction

The economic and political evolution of the Third World countries has brought to light contradictory trends which challenge the development models pursued over the last few decades, and justify a critical revision of the concepts and premises underlying the models in question. The brutal reality is that programmes generated on the basis of prevailing theories of development in less developed countries (LDCs) have aggravated poverty rather than alleviated it.

The paradigms created by A. W. Lewis, W. W. Rostow and A. O. Hirschman (the so-called modernization theorists) are based on the 'trickle-down' effect, a mechanism that supposedly triggers off economic, social and political development. In theory, then, the effects of investments in a few sectors spread through the economy to all levels of the population, thereby creating a self-sustaining economic growth cycle and reinforcing political institutions. These theories accepted short-term worsening of income inequality as a necessary transition to long-term growth and democracy. In practice, the results have been quite different. Even when aggregate economic growth rates have been high, the distribution of the fruits of growth has not been satisfactory. Real wages and incomes of the majority of the population in developing countries have, at best, stagnated. Regional inequalities have increased: rural areas have been depleted as young workers migrated to the cities in search of better jobs. The rural areas lost their most productive workers and the population at large suffered because food production diminished.

Overburdened and underfunded, local administrations in the cities are ill-equipped to cope with the waves of migrants. Shanty towns have emerged, slum areas have spread and basic services such as health, education, housing and transportation have deteriorated. Finally, those who have most benefited from the aggregate growth of the gross national product (GNP), the upper and middle classes, instead of strengthening democratic institutions as theory would suggest, have supported repressive military governments whose development and wage policies have worsened income disparities. Instead of strengthening democracy, development programmes based on the 'trickle-down' paradigm have contributed to social unrest and upheavals.

The Dependency School of development,[1] unlike the 'trickle-down' theories, acknowledges more realistically the links between the development of industrialized countries and the underdevelopment in LDCs. This school emphasizes a link established by the international division of labour between the economic achievements of the 'centre' (the industrialized nations) and those of the 'periphery' (the developing world), with the former reaping the benefits of technological progress and the latter left with primary-sector activities.

Like the trickle-down theorists, however, the Dependency School emphasizes the need to transfer capital from the developed to the developing countries. However, it is more preoccupied with reducing income disparities among nation-states than between the poor and rich within developing countries.

The critical situation of the Third World countries was undoubtedly aggravated in the 1980s as a consequence of the general recession suffered by the Western economies: its impacts and repercussions were felt in all spheres of social and cultural life, including in particular the already exhausted economies and poor populations of the underdeveloped nations. The almost continuous decline in real prices of primary export goods, the deterioration of the 'terms of trade' and the dramatic increase in the cost of energy resources occurred in conjunction with the rise of interest rates and the reduction or repatriation of foreign investments. Many development projects conceived and initiated during the boom period could not be completed in the face of adverse international conditions combined with poor planning, inefficient management and corruption.

The increasing debt service which followed the rise in international interest rates proved to be an unsustainable burden for the debtor countries, suddenly transformed into exporters of capital to the rich countries.

A major conclusion is that there are structural limits to growth which programmes designed to increase aggregate national income levels will not overcome. None the less, as advocated by the Dependency School, the challenge raised by the development impasse applies to all countries, rich and poor, developed and underdeveloped. Until this is understood, the

1. See T. Dos Santos (1969), 'The Crisis of Development Theory and the Problem of Dependence in Latin America', reprinted in H. Bernstein (ed.), *Underdevelopment and Development*, p. 76, London, Penguin, 1973: 'A conditioning situation in which . . . some countries can expand through self-impulsion while others, being in a dependent position, can only expand as a reflection of the expansion of the dominant countries.'

security, stability and peace of the world will be in permanent danger from the disturbances and conflicts that spread from the most troubled parts of the 'global village'.

Large segments of the population in LDCs live in absolute poverty as a consequence of a 'savage' accumulation process whose trends will not be reversed by producing 'more'. To reduce inequality and eliminate poverty, the concept and the policies of development have to be changed, with absolute priority given to the production of goods and services reflecting the needs of the majority of the world population.[1]

How can we account for the disparity between the 'plans' and the reality, the promises and the disappointing results? It seems that the basic causes of failure in 'development' have to be seen in the light of the basic assumptions of the policies and guidelines of development theories and practices.

Conventional approaches ignore the irrationality and lack of equity in contemporary societies, and are content to press for higher aggregate growth rates, while neglecting the problems generated by an asymmetric growth process that reflects and reinforces existing social hierarchies and unequal distribution of political power. This process is reflected by the types of goods and services produced and the underlying patterns of conspicuous consumption. A hypothetical diffusion of affluent consumption patterns will not necessarily affect the prevailing structure of social and political inequality. The transformation of the established system of power and civil rights turns out to be a necessary condition in order to offer broader access to material and symbolic goods and rewards.

A new development strategy thus requires policies and programmes to promote economic and cultural growth for everyone, not only for a minority; in all places, not only in some privileged regions; and as a continuous process, not as a cycle of ephemeral prosperity and recession.

A critical review of the recent failures of different development strategies underlines the relevance of socio-political analyses of the role of industrializing élites in an era of transnational conglomerates, and of the nature and functions of the state as an actor in the process of structural adaptation. Recent historical experiences point to the fact that obstacles to development are often of a political rather than a technical nature. This is of special

1. This also seems to be the perception of the World Bank, whose President, Barber Conable, in a recent statement called for a new development policy, oriented towards the eradication of poverty and the improvement of the quality of life. Conable explicitly criticized former World Bank policies which gave priority to economic growth and were based on monetary criteria for loans and financing development projects. Under the proposed new orientation the focus would be on programmes in education, health, housing, etc.

importance in assessing the role of science and technology in the process of late development and the achievement of economic and political independence. Nevertheless, there are no universal ready-made solutions. The heterogeneity of Third World countries is such that, with respect to levels of social and technological development, for example, the blind imitation or copying of the development strategies followed by others would be useless or harmful. In determining the potential and the limits of science and technology policies as an instrument of development, it may be useful to stress that technological autonomy is the result of a cumulative and collective historical process, closely related to the cultural and educational systems of society, its ethos or life-style, and the maturity of its work-force.

In other words, if development priorities are to be directed towards the elimination of regional, social and political inequalities, it is not only for ethical reasons (social justice), but also because it will prove impossible to become effective protagonists in the microelectronic age with large segments of the population remaining illiterate and excluded from political and cultural life.

Development policies based on science and technology cannot be reduced to mere technical operations whose sole objective is to increase the efficiency or productivity of certain factors or sectors of production. If problems of development and science and technology policies are viewed in this narrow fashion, isolated from a structural and integrated analysis of society, the result is the kind of imbalances already observed and documented during the 1970s by Myrdal, Hirschman, and others. The naïve faith and optimism of the 1960s cannot be sustained in the light of the disastrous results of the 1980s. The compensatory mechanisms of the competitive market do not function in an era of transnational conglomerates and oligopolies, while the process of accumulation in the capitalist system is by nature asymmetrical and polarizing, requiring corrective action by the state.

Technological change and innovation cannot therefore have socially beneficial effects if the cultural and political contexts are not prepared to absorb and incorporate them, and to achieve the structural transformations which will be required – a process which is much more difficult and complex than a mere transfer of resources (in this case, science and technology rather than capital) from the rich to the poor as a way of correcting imbalances.

Science and technology (S&T) have had an enormous impact on reducing the burden of physical work and improving social welfare. These contributions have been made possible only by the enormous methodological power of scientific reasoning which extends the human ability to imagine and to develop alternatives. This being said, however, the development of

16

S&T is much more than the application of objective logic. It is built on a social consensus on goals and values. Science and technology exist only through human beings in action in certain contexts, and as such cannot be entirely value-free and neutral. Modern S&T are not transhistorical phenomena, based on values beyond any critical questioning; rather, they developed with the capitalist system and form an integral element thereof. Capitalist society, more than any other in the past, has advanced through the creation and development of a special type of knowledge which has been systematically applied to the production process and has become, to an unprecedented extent, a central factor of social change.

The development of S&T cannot but be affected today by the structural characteristics of the world economic and political system which fosters integration and globalization and thus makes it all the more difficult to build up an 'autonomous' national S&T infrastructure.

Contemporary production systems are based on, and bound to, a technological innovation process which has been greatly accelerated by competition and the segmentation of worldwide markets. Thus, a central feature of modern capitalism is no longer the technical division of labour or mass production, but a continuing process of 'technological innovation' which is best achieved by 'flexible production' methods and whose demands stimulate the progress of science.

The experience of this century seems to confirm the truism that it is impossible to construct a society based on social justice and harmony upon foundations of generalized scarcity. On the other hand, there is also ample proof that there is no automatic process which ensures that overall material affluence will establish, in a given society, conditions of social well-being and equilibrium.

Accustomed as we are to a Manichean vision of the world that clearly separates good and evil, light and dark, life and death, we are unprepared to understand the dynamics of a system that simultaneously produces wealth and poverty. Yet it is essential to understand the vital need to reorganize the national and international economy in order to foster a more even distribution of costs and benefits with respect to environmental impacts and the integration of the 'backward' regions with those considered to be highly industrialized.

The following report must thus be read against this general background of some of the most burning problems of today, which are not explicitly its subject but which are among the major concerns underlying our discussion:
How to reorganize the global economy, overturning the current polarizing tendency between wealth and misery, in order to ensure a more equitable distribution of the rewards of labour.
How to put a stop to the recurrent attempts to curtail the liberty of indivi-

duals and the free expression of civil societies threatened by authoritarian governments or sterile bureaucracies.

How to avoid impoverishment, the hunger and the diseases of an ever-expanding contingent of humanity, in the face of spectacular increases in the volume of productive output and of productivity.

How to ensure that – as a result of unemployment, and the lack of access to education, culture and mass politics – basic human rights do not remain the privilege of a minority.

Science and technology can obviously contribute to these ends. Yet it must be clearly understood that they will be put to use by individuals and groups moved by interests, passions, faith or ideologies. As a result, the solution of problems will never be purely scientific and technological. When solutions emerge, they will necessarily reflect a complex blend of historical, contextual, social, economic, scientific and technological factors.

But science and technology will often – and perhaps increasingly so – turn out to be at the source of the problems to be tackled, either as by-products of scientific and technological development, or as consequences of previous choices and strategies. Effective use of S&T resources will call for systematic reassessment of past policies, taking account of their costs as well as their benefits. For example, large technological facilities may entail economies of scale, while a system of smaller ones may provide better vectors for the diffusion of innovation, but may also be difficult to manage.

The key problem here – which each country must approach from its own specific perspective – is to chart a course in order to avoid the pitfalls of excessive relocation and decentralization (with the potential risk of multiplying inconsistent actions), and excessive centralization of management (which may stifle creative initiatives). In other words, to strike a course which minimizes the risk of economic and even technological disaster on the one hand, and paralysis on the other.

It is along these lines that the following analyses, proposals and recommendations attempt to bring to light the ways in which S&T could contribute to a new phase of development. The central focus of our discussions is necessarily those countries that have already acquired an S&T research potential which must be managed and exploited – and this orientation explains why our examples are frequently drawn from experiences in Latin America, where many countries find themselves half-way between the newly industrialized countries (NICs) and those nations that still need to develop an S&T base.

This being said, our analysis aims at presenting suggestions and recommendations addressed at developing countries and taking account of their specific circumstances in order to outline strategies for the development and exploitation of S&T. These suggestions and recommendations are set out in the Conclusion.

They are, however, based on the consideration of a number of essential factors: a review of the international context which outlines the scope for government intervention in light of emerging world economic trends (Chapter 1); an assessment of the relevance of new technologies for development strategies which will bring to light new opportunities and constraints governments need to consider (Chapter 2); the exploration of alternative scenarios for the future, taking into account the broad range of achievements of developing countries in acquiring a S&T base (Chapter 3); and the major policy challenges that arise in developing copuntries and may call for new, imaginative approaches in harnessing scientific and technological opportunities to the vital requirements of development (Chapter 4).

1. The international context

The period following the Second World War brought about economic expansion at unprecedented levels; as well as a marked trend towards integration of world markets. The problems which appeared in the 1970s – currency instability due to the devaluation of the dollar, the oil crisis, falling rates of productivity growth and increasing levels of unemployment – persisted into the 1980s and had dramatic effects on the Third World countries.

Even a superficial overview of the present situation and prevailing trends makes it clear that fundamental restructuring of the world economy and society, a process in which science and technology will play an increasingly important role, is unavoidable. We shall comment briefly on the emerging polycentric geo-political constellation and its most dynamic actors.

More than 100 nation-states have emerged in the post-war period, partially offsetting the pervasive integration fostered by transnational corporations and conglomerates. None the less, the threats of economic recession, unsustainable foreign debts, high inflation rates, political unrest and institutional instability will characterize the frame of reference for the future of Third and Fourth World countries during the 1990s. In addition, major shifts taking place worldwide will affect developed and developing countries alike: uncertainty of short- and long-term economic prospects; increasing interdependence of national economies through the expansion of world trade, economic integration and the creation of new world technologies (such as telecommunications); globalization of major problems (such as the environment) which call for global responses.

This volatile environment often makes it difficult, if not impossible, to take full advantage worldwide of the opportunities generated by science and technology. The undeniable trend towards the internationalization of the world economy is thus not a linear and regular process. It is accompanied by contradictions and conflicts of interest opposing different economic and political actors and institutions.

And yet, in very concrete terms, we are entering the end of the era of bipolarity – a long period of a divided world of competing power and influence, dominated by the United States and the Soviet Union. The defeat of the world's most powerful military apparatus in Viet Nam and the withdrawal of Soviet troops from Afghanistan reflect the end of the military hegemony of the two superpowers, and their inability to impose unpopular governments *manu militari* – or, as evidenced in the immediate aftermath of the Gulf War, to obtain a change of government in a militarily defeated country. This shift is underlined by a gradual loss of economic influence and domination in both imperial systems. Although much of the attention currently focuses on changes in the centrally planned economies, the United States has also shown clear signs of economic deterioration as evidenced by falling rates of productivity and declining international competitiveness: a recent study by the Massachusetts Institute of Technology (MIT) found only two internationally competitive sectors – chemical products and aircraft – while steel, machine tools, automobiles, electronic products and even computers were losing ground in comparison with Japan and Germany. The relative decline of the American and Soviet empires has as its counterpart the emergence of new gravitational centres which attract developed and developing economies into their orbits.

In the Pacific region, after the post-war reconstruction of its industrial plants and infrastructure, the Japanese economy expanded its commercial and financial operations with the newly industrialized countries (NICs) – the four 'dragons', and the Philippines, Thailand, Malaysia and Indonesia – with the OECD member countries (New Zealand and Australia), and made inroads into the enormous potential of the Chinese market. A closer association between Japanese technology and capital with Chinese human and natural resources may displace the main financial-commercial axis from the Atlantic to the Pacific shores.

On the other side of the Pacific, the United States economy is advancing rapidly towards a closer association with the Canadian market, at the same time incorporating, through southern-border, *'maquiladora'* industries – the low-cost labour force of Mexican origin.

In Western Europe, members of the European Economic Community (EEC), including Spain and Portugal, represent a vast integrated economic and political market area of more than 300 million inhabitants. In spite of difficulties and obstacles to integration, 1992 was established as the year for the abolition of all major restrictions to free circulation of goods, capital and human resources among the member countries. However, the EEC now faces a period of adaptation as a result of political and economic changes in the Eastern European countries, and these countries, in turn, now face the challenge of redesigning their fundamental political and economic structures, as well as their international relations in all spheres.

The emerging polycentric economic and political constellations are far from moving towards the universal elimination of all frontiers, or the 'global village'. Rather, competition and tensions between the blocs may increase, while the destiny of those countries which remain excluded from the regional associations and alliances (Latin America, Africa, the Indian subcontinent, etc.) becomes uncertain and problematic. A further complicating factor in the process of geopolitical reorganization of the world economy is the overwhelming presence of transnational corporations (TNCs), with strategies and interests that diverge from nation-states' aspirations for sovereignty and sustainable development. A recent report by the United Nations Centre for Studies on Transnational Corporations reveals that about 1,000 conglomerates control more than half of the world's production and almost two-thirds of international trade. The conglomerates continue their growth and expansion even in periods of recession and crisis, through mergers and the incorporation of small competitors. The organizational culture and financial capacity of the TNCs enable them to plan and produce, trade goods and services, and undertake financial transactions and technology transfer on a global scale. The TNCs are able to restructure entire manufacturing branches and to ride the wave of new technological advances (in particular in information and communications technologies) in order to create new 'comparative advantages' – and thereby increase their profits – while the costs related to environmental degradation are borne by society. A great wave of horizontal integration is currently developing worldwide, and thus affecting industry at large. It is based on unprecedented opportunities for international management of capital and know-how, and exploits the benefits of 'just-in-time' management based on the development of integrated networks.

The enormous liquid assets manipulated by the home-country executive boards result not only in enormous returns on investments and windfall profits through financial and foreign-currency speculations, but also in strong political influence (and pressure power) on host country governments and societies characterized by little social cohesion and solidarity.

As noted above, however, the trend towards integration of the world economy through the irresistible thrust of TNCs is accompanied by another historical trend: the creation of more than 100 new nation-states in the post-war period. Born out of liberation wars or separatist movements, these new member countries of the United Nations Organization are weak in terms of military power, organization and resources. Their aspiration towards political sovereignty and economic and cultural independence are challenged, on the one hand, by the 'internationalizing' tendency of TNCs and, on the other, by the rising demands of specific ethnic groups.

In the face of these contradictory trends, and in spite of TNC demands for deregulation and liberalization of the economy, trade, foreign currency and technology policies, it is not surprising that there is a growing wave of protectionism and state intervention in almost all spheres of the economy, especially in the fields of industrial and technology policies. Even the United States Congress recently decided to increase subsidies for exports, to prohibit control of American firms by foreigners whenever 'national security' may be endangered, and to limit sales of high-tech products to potential competitors.

Protectionism and trade restrictions tend to exclude countries and regions from the benefits of expanding global trade, and thus aggravate their already declining or stagnant flows of international trade, resulting in insolvency for many peripheral countries. Even though some of these countries try hard to increase their output of raw materials and agricultural or manufactured products, the rising protectionism and neo-mercantilist policies practised by governments make it difficult to find markets to sell their goods. The export-oriented industrializing strategy adopted by several NICs created strong competition for markets in developed countries, with a consequent decline in prices of commodities. Protectionist and restrictive measures against imports were multiplied during the 1980s, as described by a United Nations document: 'A new protectionist style is emerging, more sectorial in its scope, more discriminating and less transparent. Directed against certain suppliers, and certain products, it is based on non-tariff mechanisms.' The combination of protectionist policies and technological innovations represents a serious threat to the existing comparative advantages of exporting NICs. Developed countries concentrate their exports increasingly in high-tech products while NICs continue to offer low-technology products. The eventual exports of a range of microelectronic goods by some of the Far Eastern NICs do not alter the fact that almost all integrated circuits, CAD/CAM, NCMT and robots continue to be manufactured by the United States, Japan and Western Europe. On the other hand, the continuous decline in commodities prices – a consequence of the profound recession – affects all Third World countries. Given the recessionist trends in the developed countries, it is hard to foresee a rise in prices of primary products – the main activity of peripheral economies and an important factor in their growth process.

Another negative aspect of the ongoing reorganization is the increasing substitution for natural raw materials of synthetic products developed and produced in industrialized countries. Thus the production of synthetic fibres, rubber, plastics, ceramics and alloys exerts strong downward pressure on prices of conventional raw materials produced and exported by Third World countries. The resulting unfavourable 'terms of trade' complicate even more the efforts to achieve a trade surplus or an equilibrium in the balance of payments, a prerequisite for economic reconstruction in developing countries. Due to the unstable political situation in many Third World countries, internal savings are channelled into speculative financial markets or hoarding of gold and foreign currency, thus drastically reducing the level of productive investments. Moreover, foreign capital investments have stopped flowing to LDCs, as a consequence of their indebtedness and inability to offer interest payments to international creditors, while increasing demands for credits on the part of Eastern European countries are expected to reduce still more the volume of liquidities available for developing countries.

Furthermore, the patterns of plant location that result from restructuring by TNCs create an integrated network of production premises, offices, agencies, etc. embracing the main economic and financial centres of the world market. The 'comparative advantages' of each country or region are viewed as a link in a production process deployed on a global scale, and manufacturing units of components or final assembly lines are installed, closed down or transferred according to the political and economic conditions of the respective host countries. The very flexibility and efficiency of transnational capital which assures its holders high rates of return and accumulation may thus become a factor of instability and economic decline in LDCs, as illustrated by the trajectory of a great number of export processing zones (EPZs).

During the 1960s and 1970s, a relatively small number of countries received a substantial volume of investments by TNCs, channelled into the production of basic and intermediate industrial goods characterized by the high input of raw materials, energy and labour, which are cheap and abundant factors in the NICs. The production of these outputs has become difficult or impossible in the industrialized countries due to the exhaustion of natural resources (coal, iron ore, hydroelectric potential) as well as the steady upward pressure on wages and the post-1973 rise in oil prices. Furthermore, given the increasing wave of protest against environmental pollution, almost non-existent at that time in the Third World, the choice of NICs as recipients of substantial investments was obvious. Possible increases in transportation costs of components from the different manufacturing units to the final assembly lines were more than compensated by 'transfer-pricing'.

However, the crisis of the industrial system is not a transient phenomenon. The industrial paradigm which emerged at the beginning of this century, characterized by large production units manufacturing standardized consumer goods for relatively homogeneous mass markets, is going through a profound transformation due to technological innovations and new forms of organization of work. In the conventional paradigm, the great volume of mass production required dedicated machinery and equipment, rigid specialization of tasks and labour operations, as formulated in Taylor's 'time and motion' study. Co-ordination was achieved by an authoritarian hierarchic management system, but the development of a complex mechanism of industrial relations with labour rights defended by strong and militant trade unions enabled the model to work well, to win the world wars, to maintain peace and to expand throughout the capitalist world. The first signals of vulnerability began to emerge with the spectacular advance of the Japanese industries, which surpassed their North American counterparts in efficiency and quality and conquered the leadership of some of the most dynamic sectors of the international economy based on high-tech innovations.

Evidence points to the emergence of a new industrial-technological paradigm which supersedes the installations, equipment and work processes of the 'Fordist' era. The implications and consequences of this transformation must be carefully analysed by NICs and LDCs when defining strategies and guidelines for their industrial and technological policies. The fundamental characteristics of the new paradigm – systemic integration, flexibility and incremental innovation based on the integration of microelectronics – alter established rules and competitive relationships throughout the international economy, opening up opportunities for 'leapfrogging' by LDCs, which may no longer have to face the huge fixed-capital investments of the previous Fordist paradigm based on electro-mechanical machinery.

The new techno-industrial system

Flexible specialization is a new concept that has emerged from research in advanced industrial economies. It may be of great relevance for industrial development in Third World countries, should their entrepreneurs and governments not be content merely to play the role of producers and exporters of components for mass production, but prefer instead to strive to gain a share of investments in flexible specialization and high-tech industries that would otherwise concentrate in the medium developed countries (MDCs).

Lessons must be drawn from the general recession which has spread throughout the capitalist world since the early 1970s and has had a dramatic impact on developing countries as a result of escalating debt-service payments accompanied by declining export revenues. In spite of the great diversity of political and technological abilities, some generic observations can be made on this basis.

First of all, automated machines and equipment have not been and will continue not to be the decisive factors in competitiveness and the conquest of foreign markets. Intangible investments (ranging from basic technical skills to sophisticated marketing abilities, and including engineering and R&D) have been shown time and again to play a decisive role in this respect. A number of recent studies point out that changes in the organizational structure, management practices and work processes are the basic pre-condition for the successful incorporation of new technologies. Instead of exaggerated concern with embodied technologies (hardware), the main efforts ought to be directed towards: (a) the systemic integration of the whole manufacturing process; (b) improvement of material and component supply-systems; (c) the reduction of inventories by 'just-in-time' organization; (d) changes in design and work processes, to facilitate 'design for manufacture'; (e) better quality control procedures; (f) economies of 'scope' and not only of scale; (g) reduction of energy and raw-material consumption; and (h) upgrading and training of the labour force.

The essence of the new industrial paradigm, whose implications for developing countries will be discussed in greater detail in Chapter 2, is not a fully automated plant but a management system which creates a process that continuously absorbs incremental or secondary innovations leading to higher levels of efficiency and competitiveness. In other words, modern and sophisticated technologies do not replace, but rather depend on, a qualified, well-trained and motivated labour force. It is not cheap labour, but small and continuous technological advances based on imagination, motivation, technical and organizational creativity that represent the competitive advantage. Unless the introduction of new machines and equipment is preceded and accompanied by the reorganization and decentralization of production facilities and decision-making, production costs may increase. The reorganization may cause the disarticulation and even the obstruction of conventional production lines.

In the industrialized countries, there is an overall trend away from the 'Fordist' paradigm characterized by rigid and dedicated production lines and the manufacture of standardized goods for large markets. The increasing oligopolization of the markets resulted in only marginal increases of demand, while building up barriers to the entry of new competitors. With the exhaustion of potential primary or radical innovations, competition between oligopolies takes place less by cost reduction than through new packages and design differentiation. North American firms have concentrated their R&D efforts on radical innovations expected to result in new levels of technological sophistication. By ignoring the organizational aspects, they have fallen behind the more dynamic Japanese corporations whose policies and guidelines have combined incremental innovations with new organizational forms and human resources management, affecting strategic planning on the plant as well as on the corporate level in its operation on global markets.

The key element of this restructuring process is flexibility, based on multi-purpose machinery production units which allow for automated production of small batches by the use of reprogrammable equipment. Thus, it becomes possible to change easily from one product to another – a difficult process when using dedicated machinery – and also to obtain economies of scope by increasing the number of batches of different manufactured products.

Competition for markets in advanced industrial societies requires customer-oriented, small-batch production without completely abandoning the manufacture of standardized mass products. However, as these production and assembly lines become more flexible, the qualification and training of managers and workers, and industrial relations on plant and sectorial levels, are profoundly affected. The new paradigm does not depend exclusively on automated machinery which can be utilized in rigid as well as in flexible systems. It is characterized by flexibility combined with systemic integration, in opposition to the conception and practices of the Fordist-Taylorist model, dominant during the greater part of this century. The characteristics of the new paradigm, as suggested by Perez (1983), include:

A strong tendency towards information or knowledge intensity, as opposed to material and energy intensity, predominant in the conventional industrial production paradigm.

The emergence of flexibility as the main characteristic of the manufacturing process, thereby challenging the traditional concept of economies of scale as a necessary condition for productivity increases.

The diffusion of a new concept of organizational efficiency, based on 'systematization' rather than on automation.

The systemic organization generates a closer relationship between markets and manufacturing centres and is based on dynamic monitoring rather than on rigid and periodical planning. Consequently, there emerges a new management style based on objective information rather than on intuition or subjective certainty. The new style is accompanied by control systems based on decentralized networks, to the detriment of currently dominant hierarchical bureaucracies.

These basic characteristics of the new techno-economic paradigm of the fifth Kondratieff cycle will be explored in greater detail in Chapter 2, since they will directly affect the 'windows of opportunities' which open for developing countries as a result of new technological developments. It is enough to underline at this stage that these new features may alter the rules and limits of the international economy, creating 'leap-frogging' possibilities for NICs and developing countries, which are less committed to the former paradigm due to their late industrialization process. Some of the past constraints to development, such as the access to wide markets and heavy investments in capital goods, may be overcome through the introduction and utilization of the new technologies, which offer possibilities to combine centralized large-scale production with decentralized secondary manufacturing.

These trends offer new opportunities for small- and medium-sized industries (SMIs), which represent the bulk of productive capacity in developing countries. Small firms in NICs have always had difficulties in gaining access to technology, either because of the high entry costs or the complicated process of bargaining for the transfer of technology or licensing rights from a foreign firm. Within the new paradigm, SMIs do not necessarily have to dominate all the phases of a given manufacturing process. While small firms individually cannot attain flexible specialization, they can compensate for their individual weakness by sectorial association. The important point is that equipment, components and different services ought to be available on the local level, leading thereby to the sectorial agglomeration of firms, which in turn has positive repercussions on the regional economy. Recent experiences in developed countries support the thesis that sectorial agglomeration is more likely to occur in relatively small- or medium-sized urban areas as opposed to the diseconomies-generating metropolis. Emphasis and priority in development programmes and projects, within the paradigm of systemic integration and flexible specialization, ought to be based on clustering (co-operatives, consortia) of SMIs and a well-developed inter-firm division of labour through subcontracting and the provision of specialized expertise and output.

The basic underlying principle is expressed by the notion of 'collective efficiency' applied to a locally and vertically integrated industrial structure, which enhances its capacity to deal with changes in the market. While the collective efficiency of the work-force becomes more important than control over the individual worker's performance, over-emphasized by Taylorist practices of separating conception from execution of work, labour has to be treated as a resource to be developed over time rather than as a cost item to be reduced in the short term. The same concept can be applied to a cluster of small firms which, through systemic integration and incremental innovations assisted by university-based R&D centres, are able to increase significantly their collective efficiency and hence their economic performance.

Such an approach is of the highest relevance for industrialization in developing countries. The extent to which they will be able to embark on flexible specialization and systemic integration depends on the specific structural and political conditions of each society as much as on the specific policies of their governments. In spite of unprecedented integration into the world economy, most LDCs seem unable to enter, either by their own efforts or by conventional international Keynesian policies, a new era of economic growth and expansion. Some LDCs will need different degrees of structural adjustment while others may require more than marginal changes. The increasing evidence that there is no unique road to development gives support to the request for additional theoretical and empirical studies on differentiation and polarization during the dynamic process of capital accumulation and integration on a global scale.

Without engaging in speculative forecasts, one may assume that the next decade will require a high degree of adjustment and structural changes of LDC economies in order to survive as politically viable entities. The capacity to adapt to international competition, with its disruptive impacts on internal markets, can best be developed in clusters or associations of SMIs sharing a common sectorial and regional interest. The decisive factor continues to be governmental, industrial and technological policies on the macro level, especially with regard to the size of the internal market.

Flexible specialization capacity and systemic integration will lead to a significant increase in collective efficiency or productivity in meeting potential and unsatisfied demand, achieving higher levels of consumption and improving the quality of life at all levels of society. This kind of restructuring of industry obviously cannot be left to individual initiatives or market forces alone.

Government intervention through the selective financing and co-ordination of adjustment efforts, at local, regional or national levels, will turn out to be a necessary condition for any viable strategy of sustainable growth. In addition, efforts to increase collective efficiency through regional integration and closer international co-operation between developing countries, may prove all the more necessary in the present context of multipolarization of the world economy.

Developing countries are thus entering a difficult and important transition phase which cannot be successfully bridged on the basis of minimal and incremental change. The major challenges stem from the multiplication of major discontinuities resulting from political, economic and technological changes. Consensual approaches will be required to prevent whole societies from being left behind. But developing countries can take advantage of some of the most important features of the new techno-economic system: its major opportunities can be seized on the basis

30

of new learning harnessed to the original and dynamic creation of new products and processes. There is a definite advantage, in this light, in having a limited industrial heritage whose dead weight would stifle creative forces.

2. The relevance of new technologies

Chapter 1 outlined the major discontinuities and constraints which characterize the new international environment at the beginning of the 1990s. The following argument will extend this analysis in a long-term view of economic growth, essentially based on a Schumpeterian perspective.

We consider that, since the early 1970s, the world has entered a period of volatile and turbulent transition towards a new phase of socio-economic development, in which the diffusion of a host of interrelated new technologies, institutions and forms of organization could lead to a renewed period of economic growth and prosperity. Profound changes are taking place in science and technology which will set the new phase of development in entirely new quantitative and qualitative dimensions, once they spread throughout economic systems. We argue that the beginning of such a diffusion phase, in which the ultimate characteristics of the future development trajectory are being shaped, could constitute an opportunity window for reducing development disparities between countries. We also consider that successful catching up will require the effective introduction and diffusion of the various elements of the emerging new development regime rather than the pursuit of past strategies.

This argument will be illustrated with examples drawn from emerging energy, transport and communication technologies. These examples will in particular bring to light the importance of participation in international flows of technical knowledge, skills and capital in order to make more effective and better use of the growth (and catch-up) opportunities opened up by the diffusion of a new socio-technical 'bandwagon'. We shall argue on the basis of historical examples that heterogeneity with regard to socio-technical options as well as to patterns of diffusion or resource consumption has been, and will continue to be, an essential strategic asset for developing countries. As such we refute the prescriptive character of scenarios which assume that diffusion and resulting resource-consumption levels realized in a previous expansion phase remain realistic (even desirable) goals for sub-sequent periods.

Structural adjustments and emergence of a new socio-technical development phase

One of the basic conclusions derived from analysis of long-term economic growth and development relates to the discontinuous and disruptive nature and effects of technological and socio-institutional change. Steering away from the notion of development trajectories sailing smoothly along an equilibrium path, economic theory increasingly acknowledges the discontinuous nature of development and the existence of phases of transition to new growth trajectories. Scientific and technological innovations, as well as the socio-institutional framework, play a critical role in the transition to new growth trajectories and in defining their configurations.

The attempt to clarify these interactions often refers to the notion of long waves in economic development, which would account for the emergence of successive new forms of development and economic growth, driven by the diffusion of technologies and institutions, and interlaced with economic restructuring and transformations in social relations. This process generates the ebb-and-flow pattern of expansionary and recessionary (restructuring) periods experienced in market economies during the last two centuries. Rather than a process of continuous growth, long-wave theory supports the idea that growth itself comes in pulses stimulated by the appearance and widespread diffusion of social, institutional and technological innovations, leading to new forms of organization of production, new products, new infrastructures and even whole new industries.

Although there is no unanimous agreement about the theoretical and empirical underpinnings of this model of long-term economic growth, there is consensus that technological change and the socio-institutional forces shaping the characteristics and adoption modes of innovations can no longer be treated merely as residual factors of economic growth and development, but are its central driving forces.

Innovation should thus be viewed as a complex social process extending far beyond changes in products and processes. What is at stake here is the growth potential of an interrelated set of technological innovations and associated 'best' engineering and management practices, which can only be realized in conjunction with the acquisition of new skills and the creation of new organizational forms in production and social relations. Technological advances and socio-institutional innovations interact to produce major economic upturns which have pervasive effects throughout the economy and society – a model frequently referred to as 'techno-economic paradigms'.

In this light, periods of economic expansion can be seen as driven by sets of interrelated social and technical innovations. In each particular development phase, a dynamic blend of major technological and organizational innovations raises the levels of productivity and degree of economic development which had been possible (sustainable) under a previous development regime.

Such a new development regime will emerge, however, only through a process of restructuring prompted by the exhaustion of the growth potential of the previously dominant form and direction of economic growth, i.e. in response to the fact that a particular phase of economic expansion approaches saturation when reaching a number of limits (market, environmental, social acceptance, etc.) and thus becomes increasingly characterized by diminishing returns, increasing disbenefits, and an accelerating pattern of incremental innovations. In other words, it will tend to appear in industrialized countries which have exhausted the growth potential of old technologies, and not in LDCs, which have not.

The new development (growth) regime in industrialized countries thus pushes back the limits of market saturation and further productivity increases which constrain the previous dominant mode of economic growth and development. The full-scale realization of the new growth potentials cannot however be fully realized without major restructuring and far-reaching social and institutional changes. It entails, for example, the development of new technologies and products, the rise and decline of entire industries and infrastructures, changes in the international division of labour, and relocation of industries and technological leadership. It also calls for transformations in: (a) the skills and composition of the work-force; (b) the education and training system; (c) the system of industrial relations; (d) the structure (e.g. level of integration) of firms; (e) production and management 'styles' and practices; (f) the international trading and financial system; etc. The widespread diffusion of new technologies, products and institutions ushers in a new development regime which in turn opens the way for an economic upturn and a period of economic growth.

This process is an international phenomenon, which is reflected in a wave-like, broadly synchronous movement of aggregate indicators such as diffusion of technologies, clusters of technologies and infrastructures, industrial outputs and prices, etc. We may assume that an event simultaneously affecting the economic and social evolution of a number of core countries at a particular development phase will most likely have common roots and will have worldwide repercussions, thus affecting fringe countries as well. This holds not only for growth periods, but even more so for the downswing and recessionary periods marking the transition between two consecutive growth or development regimes.

The emergence and subsequent diffusion of innovations heralding a new development phase will take place in a context of intensive restructuring, which is 'sudden' in generating price instabilities in the energy and primary commodity markets and turbulence in financial markets, 'destructive' in the saturation of traditional markets and products, and the resulting slowdown of economic growth rates, and – last but not least – in the dislocation and obsolescence effects on skills, comparative economic advantage and capital (including large-scale destruction of speculative capital). Yet, at the same time, it is 'creative' in the development of innovations, new skills and capital and thus in its capacity to generate new products, services and growth sectors.

The key point here is that the period of restructuring provides an opportunity window for followers to catch up even though the conditions for spontaneous adjustment to the new development paradigm could not be met at an earlier stage. For example, at the early stage of formation of a new development regime, local skill levels can still be translated into new value-generating activities and products with relatively modest capital outlays, as opposed to the import of capital-intensive mature technologies and goods production facilities, say in the form of large-scale integrated steel plants, textile industry and so on, which have traditionally been taken to be areas of comparative advantage for developing and newly industrialized countries. It may also even be considered that followers have a certain strategic advantage in such transition periods as they have no heavy commitment – in terms of capital vintage structure, infrastructures, level and composition of skills and organizational/institutional settings – to the previously dominant (and progressively vanishing) mode of economic growth.

Elements of a possible new growth phase

The economic growth phase that followed the Second World War was associated with a cluster of interrelated technical and managerial innovations, leading to productivity levels clearly superior to those attainable with previous technologies (primarily based on coal and steam power) and forms of organization of production systems. In particular, the extension of the continuous flow concept of the chemical industry to the mass production of identical units made with energy-intensive materials enabled unprecedented real-term cost and price decreases and thus opened an era of mass consumption based on products such as the internal-combustion engine and the automobile, petrochemicals, plastics and consumer durables, and many others. Petroleum played a vital role, due to its availability at low cost and to its role of principal energy carrier and feedstock in the industry, residential and transport sectors. The prototype of the corresponding production organization was the Fordist assembly line, complemented at organizational level by a separation of management and administration from production in accordance with Taylorist ideas of scientific management.

This technological 'style' was matched by the social and institutional framework which emerged after a period of deep economic depression and social turmoil in the 1930s. Evidence suggests that there is once again a widening 'mismatch' between the socio-institutional framework of a particular phase of economic growth and the attainment of limits (market, environmental, social acceptance, etc.) to its further expansion, and the emergence of a new development phase as represented in changing social values, new technologies and growth sectors, new forms of production organization, shifts in the occupational profiles and the international relative cost advantages.

In the previous development phase, productivity increases were primarily obtained by increasing economies of scale in the mass production of energy- and material-intensive products. We argue that the new phase of economic expansion will call for advances in systems integration, flexibility and quality, environmental compatibility, value- and information-intensive (but increasingly material- and energy-saving) products, and the creation of a production system in which the whole philosophy of 'just-in-time' production, high turn-round times and inventory reduction, unprecedented quality and precision levels, etc., will become dominant. Productivity increases will no longer be based on economies of scale, but rather on economies of scope.

The following discussion focuses on some technological elements of a possible new development phase, in the light of emerging new tendencies in the fields of energy, manufacturing and, finally, transport and communication.

The availability of technology alone, however, is not a sufficient condition for a renewed period of economic growth and expanding development opportunities. These are contingent on the mediating socio-institutional factors: the embedding of technologies in the economic and social system in general and, more particularly, the availability of appropriate economic incentives (e.g. low interest rates which encourage productive investment) and of human skills. The latter cannot be analysed comprehensively in the following discussion, but their critical importance must be emphasized before we address some of the emerging technology clusters which might become more and more pervasive in the next phase of development.

ENERGY

Extreme price volatility since the beginning of the 1970s has made energy the focus of attention of analysts, policy-makers and the general public. The most important characteristics of the 1970s and 1980s in this area has been the structural transition in the primary energy supply mix, with the market dominance of petroleum (and the oil-producers' cartel, OPEC) having reached its zenith and starting to decline, if only in relative market share terms, and the apparent decoupling of energy from general economic growth. These shorter-term developments should not, however, overshadow longer-term trends in the evolution of the energy system. In particular, the transition to new energy carriers has never been due to resource scarcity as such: it was not the scarcity of fuel-wood (as even today's global energy consumption could theoretically be met by the global annual wood-reproduction rate) that led to the transition to coal beginning in the eighteenth century, and it was not the lack of resources and sources of supply that led to the transition away from coal to oil, after the mid nineteenth century. The driving forces were higher quality, energy density and thus improved possibilities for transportation and storage, versatility and ease of use, as well as the emergence of new applications, which led to the transition to new forms of energy carriers.

The transition from wood to coal, from coal to oil and the present transition away from oil were thus not caused by resource scarcity but by the better compatibility of new energy vectors with changing social, economic and environmental requirements, as well as by the boundary conditions of evolving societies. Structural change in the global primary energy mix made it possible to achieve ever higher energy efficiencies while tackling urgent environmental issues. The transition from fuel wood and charcoal to coal resolved the problems of deforestation in areas close to the main centres of consumption. It was not until the transition away from coal that the infamous London smog finally disappeared. The replacement of horses by the automobile at the beginning of this century resolved in a similar way an urgent problem of urban pollution – horse manure. In turn, the massive spread of car-ownership after the Second World War resulted in a new impact on the environment, which is (by the introduction of catalytic converters) only now beginning to be adequately resolved.

From this longer-term view, we argue that further increases in energy efficiency, improved environmental compatibility, enhanced system integration and robustness and, finally, increasing flexibility, safety and quality of energy carriers, will evolve as crucial factors, as opposed to considerations of security and geo-politics reflecting the 'Malthusian myths' of resource and supply constraints, which were considered as the main driving forces for the future in the aftermath of the oil crisis of the 1970s.

These driving forces become all the more important in view of two major trends which increasingly affect the energy sector. The first lies in the increasing globalization of environmental issues, in particular the increase in atmospheric carbon dioxide concentrations and the possibility of significant climate changes, as opposed to the more local (urban smog) and regional (especially acid rain) concerns which have thus far dominated scientific and policy discussions. The second trend (or rather likely hypothesis) deals with the future evolution of energy prices in general and that of oil in particular. We argue that the hypothesis that energy price levels will remain stable and relatively low on a real-term basis over the medium-term time horizon (e.g. over the next twenty years) no longer appears to be a mere possibility, but instead rather likely. This is because of further improvements in efficiency of energy use, the emergence of value- and information-intensive (as opposed to material- and energy-intensive) products as core elements of a possible new economic upswing, as well as the considerable potential for further technological improvements (and cost reductions) at all steps of the energy chain from exploration and production to end use.

As a result of technological developments in all these areas, the availability of natural-gas reserves has already increased dramatically. Whereas natural-gas reserves accounted in 1970 for only half of the petroleum reserves, they have now reached parity. Reserve to production ratios exceed fifty-eight years globally and even eighty years for non-OPEC developing countries. Since 1970, net reserve additions have grown nearly three times faster than the increase in gas demand and, as shown in Table 1, natural-gas finds have been particularly noteworthy in developing countries (increase by more than a factor of six since 1970). Large potentials for further gas finds, particularly in those countries not endowed with petroleum fields, apparently exist. Over 100 countries at present have identified commercially viable gas reserves. However, in a number of countries (sixteen in Africa alone with total gas reserves in excess of 900 billion m^3 of natural gas, that is, over ninety years of the African continent's present gas production, excluding OPEC members Algeria and Nigeria), exploitation of identified gas deposits has not yet started owing to the lack of appropriate transport and end-use infrastructures. The lack of appropriate infrastructure in some oil-producing developing countries even leads to considerable waste. Nigeria, for instance, in 1986 flared 75 per cent of its associated natural-gas production due to lack of facilities for re-injection and transport.

The large identified gas reserves in many oil-importing developing countries would thus argue for increased utilization of natural gas and a sig-

TABLE I. Natural-gas reserves and production (1970–88) in 10^9 m^3

Region	Reserves		Production		Ratio 1988/1970	
	1970	1988	1970	1988	Reserves	Production
North America	9 236	8 040	685	546	0.87	0.80
Western Europe	4 118	5 416	77	196	1.32	2.55
USSR and Eastern Europe	9 516	42 481	232	793	4.46	3.42
Japan, Australia and New Zealand	560	2 469	4	20	4.41	5.00
OPEC	12 619	39 870	38	185	3.16	4.87
Subtotal	36 076	98 276	1 036	1 740	2.72	1.86
Non-OPEC developing countries[1]	2 022	12 407	41	151	6.14	3.68
World[2]	38 098	110 683	1 077	1 891	2.91	1.76

1. Reserve/production ratio: 1970, 49.3 years; 1988, 82.2 years.
2. Reserve/production ratio: 1970, 35.4 years; 1988, 58.5 years.

Source: CEDIGAZ, 1985, 1988.

nificant share of gas in the energy balance of the countries concerned. However, the fact that many developing countries (particularly in Africa) have not been able to obtain sufficient technological and financial assistance for the development of their national energy endowments raises a number of questions about the adequacy of present policies of financial assistance in the energy sector of developing countries. We cannot help but question policies which provide funding for oil imports but no sufficient means to reduce imports by exploiting abundant natural-gas reserves. Appropriate mechanisms for technical assistance and especially for financing hydrocarbon (in particular natural gas) exploration, as well as the development of the infrastructure needed for efficient use of this resource in developing countries even under conditions of low energy prices will have to be vigorously developed.

Important market potentials for increased use of natural gas exist in both industrialized and developing countries: in the industry sector (e.g. fertilizer production), households (bottled liquid natural gas), even in the transport sector (e.g. compressed natural-gas cylinders). Bottled liquid natural gas or similar commercial high-density energy carriers offer considerable energy efficiency advantages over traditional renewable fuels for cooking purposes and could help to reduce local fuel-wood shortages.

The largest potential for natural gas, however, may well be in the decentralized production of electricity based on gas turbines. From the end-use side, gas turbine technology offers particularly promising prospects in view of its flexibility, environmental compatibility and energy efficiency. Guaranteed efficiencies of 52 per cent are currently being realized (compared with about 32–34 per cent for coal, oil or nuclear power plants) and 60 per cent appears technically feasible; flat economies of scale and low initial investments are particularly advantageous for flexible, modular and decentralized applications for electricity generation, for example, in island operation mode (thus reducing the high capital requirements of electricity transmission and distribution networks associated with large-scale, investment-intensive hydropower projects). Furthermore, the development of gas turbine technology is not necessarily dependent on the availability of natural gas, since biomass (e.g. sugar-cane residues, corn stover or rice husks) can be used as fuel.

To sum up, the considerable economic and environmental advantages of natural gas (practically sulphur free, lowest nitrogen oxides and carbon dioxide emissions of all fossil fuels) can be realized in developing countries only if appropriate instruments for technology transfer and financing of exploration activities and development of the necessary transport and distribution infrastructure become available. Also, appropriate adjustments of the institutional and legal framework in developing countries will often be required. One possibility would be to offer incentives for large multinational oil companies to increase natural-gas exploration outside petroleum-producing provinces when present market conditions – especially under continuing low energy prices – most likely would not be sufficient to open the natural-gas option for developing countries other than those (already fairly numerous) where significant gas reserves have been identified to date. Another goal would be to to provide appropriate technical assistance and capital for developing a natural-gas supply and usage infrastructure in these countries.

Future development prospects of nuclear energy appear less certain at present. These prospects will reflect the extent to which it will prove possible to develop new, inherently safe reactor designs (which also ought to allow for smaller unit sizes), effective solutions to radioactive waste disposal, and appropriate institutional and social formulas for nuclear power generation.

MANUFACTURING

Mass production, mass consumption of energy, and material-intensive products have long been at the core of economic growth, particularly since the Second World War. Conventional wisdom holds that economies of scale and cost reductions via labour-saving technologies will continue to be the major future driving forces in the manufacturing sector. We argue, however, that the emerging future development trajectory will be characterized by a shift away from energy- and material-intensive products towards value- and information-intensive ones.

The social and institutional dimension may play an increasing role in the diffusion of the innovations which will pave the way to a new economic upswing. Reducing barriers to innovation, increasing flexibility, complexity and quality of the outputs of the economic system, as well as decreasing the time required between design and marketing, are probably more dependent on socio-institutional factors than on technological aspects alone. This is particularly true at a time when a host of technological innovations are on the brink of widespread diffusion into the manufacturing sector, all of which will contribute to shaping the structure and the determinants of future manufacturing activities.

One of the key technological factors in the future evolution of the manufacturing system has already emerged: low-cost micro-electronics, which open the way for flexible batch-production networks, where all activities (managerial, administrative, productive, etc.) are integrated in an information-intensive system. The concept of integration will also shift from vertical (i.e. a company engaged in all stages, from primary raw material production to final product manufacturing and marketing) to horizontal integration, that is, an increasing specialization, co-operation and eventual emergence of large specialized international companies performing specific tasks (e.g. design, marketing or specialized forms of financing).

The elements of the new emerging development phase – often referred to as the 'information and communication Kondratieff', or 'Fifth Kondratieff' – are thus technologically rooted in advances in microelectronics and photonics, which hold the promise of a quantum leap in performance and potential productivity increases, the emergence of better material-saving and energy-effective technologies (for example, the gas turbines discussed above, or electronic applications in automobiles which will reduce specific fuel consumption, or recent advances in aircraft propulsion, such as the Ultra High Bypass engine designs, etc.) as well as of technologies, such as industrial robotics, flexible manufacturing (FMS) and computer-integrated manufacturing (CIM) systems, which foster fast, flexible and extremely high-quality production of even small batch sizes. The potential range of application of these new technological developments is enormously extended by other developments, also linked to information technology, in the transportation of goods and the overall logistics chain which enable the realization of 'just-in-time' production principles and the general reduction of inventory requirements.

42

The whole philosophy of 'just-in-time' production and inventory reduction is probably best illustrated by the case of the Cadillac Allanté, a car body manufactured by Pininferina in Turin, Italy, and transported by air freight over 5,000 kilometres to General Motors in Detroit, United States, for final assembly of engine, power train and electronics. This enormous 'production line' is apparently economic, taking account of all the direct and indirect costs of potential damage, insurance and the production inventories that would be locked in ocean freighters for weeks. From such a perspective, further dematerialization (i.e. raising the value generated per kg material input) of manufactured goods and an increase in their value through higher software and information content, would tend to add to the importance of air freight transport. This is highly relevant to development prospects outside the developed economies.

A first possible consequence of the tendencies emerging in the manufacturing sector of relevance to NICs and developing countries may consist in the relocation of certain manufacturing activities (e.g. in the textile sector) back to highly developed countries. Labour-cost advantages would therefore no longer be a decisive locational advantage if quality, flexibility, small batch sizes, inventory and time reduction between design and marketing did indeed become the main driving forces in the manufacturing sector. In order to maintain a locational advantage it appears necessary to provide access to advanced communication and transport infrastructures (e.g. location of production facilities for export of manufactured goods close to airports), as well as to develop a new institutional and organizational framework. On the other hand, NICs and developing countries may still have a definite strategic advantage, since they have neither heavy commitment to, nor full implementation of, the traditional manufacturing system and the socio-institutional framework supporting it. Taking advantage of the opportunities opened by an emerging new development phase, and introducing an institutional framework supporting it, may thus turn out to be easier than in the United States, with its heavy commitment to large-scale Fordist mass production based on Tayloristic management principles, or in Europe, with its labour-market rigidities. These opportunities imply that certain threshold levels of development have been achieved, and thus may be relevant for only a limited number of developing countries.

A final point needs to be made with respect to the manufacturing sector in connection with basic industries such as steel. We have alluded above to the increasing trend towards dematerialization in terms of material consumption per unit of economic activity in developed economies (see Fig. 1). This 'dematerialization' observed for advanced economies is the result of both changes in the output mix of these economies (shift to higher-value and information-intensive products, in particular the growth of the service sector) and the availability of new materials (plastics, special alloys, composites, ceramics, etc.) which provide the same (even improved) range of services (e.g. tensile strength) with less material input (measured by weight).

The fact that the global steel market is apparently reaching saturation indicates that: (a) developed countries are moving progressively in the direction of increasing dematerialization, and (b) that follower countries, while increasing their steel output, are not likely to do so in a (quantitatively) similar way to that of the industrialized countries in the post Second World War period. This is due to the fact that the particular development trajectory (high growth in steel-intensive sectors/products such as automobiles, shipbuilding, etc.) long characteristic of prevailing patterns of economic growth is not likely to be repeated. It is not so much that the basic material sector will not continue to be important for economic development, but that its expansion (i.e. increase by a factor of seven globally since 1945) will not be the same as in the previous phase of economic growth, since the particular historic development pattern based on massive diffusion of car ownership, consumer durables, etc., is progressively giving way to a new material- and energy-extensive growth trajectory. Under conditions of saturation (or at best of only modest growth rates) of the production of basic material, the much stronger dematerialization tendencies of developed countries will result in a further shift in the relative market shares (and most likely also of absolute production capacities) of the location of

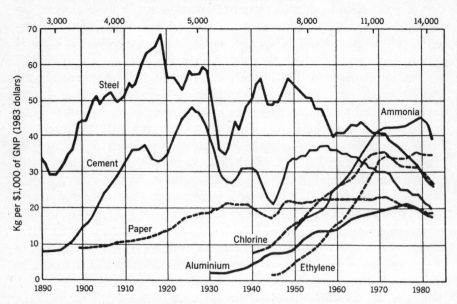

FIG. 1. Materials consumption in relation to per capita GNP in the United States (1983 dollars). After Williams et al., 1987.

basic materials production. At the same time, this production will progressively shift from large-scale integrated steel mills to more flexible and higher-quality production (including in environmental terms), based, for example, on mini-mills with recycled scrap and electric-arc furnaces, continuous casting and a shift in production to high-quality speciality products.

TRANSPORT AND COMMUNICATIONS

Two of the main trends emerging in transport and communications need to be discussed here. The first consists in a host of new technologies, allowing unprecedented levels of speed, variety and information density in communications. The second relates to the emerging new characteristics of the manufacturing sector which have been discussed above (integration, small batch-size production, increased flexibility and reduction of design to marketing lead times) and their resulting repercussions on the transport sector. Here, in particular, there will be an increasing demand for high-speed, high-quality transport systems (such as air transport) and nodes in the international transport network which provide for best integration between different modes of transportation and between the various hierarchical levels (global and international, regional, national and local) .

The possible emergence of new infrastructures (for example, very rapid trains in large urban corridors along the lines of the Japanese Shinkansen, or in connecting large air transport hubs) should be taken into account. The development of new infrastructure systems and, especially, their complementarity and integration into existing transport infrastructures emerges as an important area of strategic public infrastructure policy in the longer term, as opposed to the shorter-term tactical concerns which attempt to cope with immediate congestion problems or negative externalities (i.e. environmental pollution) associated with dense road traffic in urban areas and international transit corridors.

The introduction of new information and communication technologies multiplies the potential impacts of the driving forces which shape the future of the transport system, such as quality, including speed and environmental compatibility; flexibility and the application of 'just-in-time' principles to the whole logistics chain of transportation (including, for example, warehousing operations). These impacts become ever more pervasive in the transition to higher shares of high-value goods ('dematerialization', i.e. decrease in energy and material intensity and increase in information and software content per unit value) in the manufacturing sector.

The apparent 'dematerialization' tendencies of advanced economies as reflected in indicators of material consumption per unit of economic activity discussed above (see Fig. 1) are also mirrored in indicators of transport intensity. From a long-term perspective, industrialized countries appear to be on the brink of a major turning point, since the goods transport intensities started to decline in the early 1970s. Passenger transport intensities, on the other hand, have continued their rising trend.

The reason for the apparent 'decoupling' of goods tonnage transported per unit of economic activity in industrialized countries is obvious. It stems from the gradual transition in the output mix of these economies in the direction of information- and value-intensive (but material-extensive) products, and from the availability of higher-quality and lighter substitutes in the form of advanced materials. This transition also has important repercussions on the type and quality of transport services required for the delivery of high-value goods, since it will favour higher-quality modes of transport, with quality essentially defined in terms of flexibility (i.e. smaller shipment sizes), speed and reliability in delivery (such as truck and especially air transportation).

The availability of appropriate transport and communication infrastructures, and the ability to use them creatively, has become of ever-increasing importance for newly industrializing and developing countries in view of recent developments in the manufacturing sector and the pervasive worldwide spread of new communications and information technologies.

The emergence of new infrastructures makes it conceivable for these countries to achieve a development short-cut and save at least one step in the historical development chain of transport and communications systems, for instance by building communication networks based on integrated services digital networks (ISDNs) or high-capacity regional air-transport systems rather than a development along the lines of post Second World War mass motorization, analogue communication systems and highway construction. The technological base for such developments is attainable in some developing countries, as illustrated by a recent co-operation project between MBB of Germany and China on the development of a medium-sized (100 passengers) regional aircraft, to be produced in China. The successful Brazilian aircraft industry, producing small commuter aircraft, may serve here as another illustration that the technological base is partially developed already and does not necessarily rely on a complete import of the required technology. In some cases, when endogenous resources are not sufficient in a single country, similar developments could be promoted at regional level.

The new technologies also offer solutions to some of the perennial or emerging problems of developing countries: new ground-based, high-speed, energy-efficient mass-transit systems both at the regional level and for local traffic; the further development of urban high-capacity transit systems in developing countries in response to the rapid growth of urban areas and the extensive environmental pollution stemming from intense automobile traffic in metropolitan areas (as in the case of Mexico City and of the many other rapidly growing urban areas in the Third World).

The development and operation of such large technological systems provides many opportunities to acquire new engineering and management skills in government, industry and services.

Diffusion bandwagons and development trajectories

Specific policy conclusions can thus be drawn from an assessment of future development opportunities and prospects, in light of the diffusion of a whole new set of technological and institutional innovations, taking into account three historical characteristics of the diffusion of socio-technical systems:

The interrelatedness which defines clusters or sets of technological and institutional innovations, explaining their pervasive effects throughout the economy.

The international nature of the diffusion of innovation clusters. Core countries display an interrelated dynamic in the development of these clusters, stemming from their integration in terms of exchanges in technologies, capital and human resources; latecomers then catch up. This development will frequently result in a relatively synchronous pattern in the completion dates of the expansion of particular innovation clusters.

The broad range of variations in the ultimate diffusion levels (i.e. extent or consumption) achieved in different countries.

The development-policy implications of these essential characteristics will be better understood by reference to a specific historical example that has played a major role in economic development worldwide – railways.

INTERRELATEDNESS

The development of the railways as the dominant transport mode of the second half of the nineteenth century and first half of the twentieth century was contingent on a host of technological innovations, spanning the development of the steam engine (e.g. improving traction power), developments in: material sciences to avoid boiler explosions (quite frequent initially); steel technologies for rail fabrication; communications technologies for signalling purposes (the telegraph); fuel technologies; energy efficiency; the chemical industry; and engineering and building sciences. These many dimensions indicate the importance (and interdependence) of a whole set, or 'cluster', of technological innovations, which are required in order to develop such pervasive systems as new infrastructures. In addition, various organizational and financial innovations proved to be of vital importance for the successful construction and management of railways, in the industrializing core countries as well as in the periphery.

This illustrates the importance of interrelatedness of innovations: new infrastructure systems determine major lines of development for particular historical expansion periods, such as the age of canals, railways or the automobile (roads). The pervasive economic effects of the development of such large systems do not only stem from a variety of multiplier effects (in terms of forward and backward linkages), but also from the fact that new infrastructure systems open the way for ever higher quality of services, thus raising the productivity of economies to levels which would not have been possible by a simple intensification of use of old infrastructures.

Thus, the development of railways, for instance, has to be viewed as a fundamental qualitative leap in productivity levels, which could not be achieved by further development of traditional transport modes. This argument can be highlighted in the words of Schumpeter: 'Add as many coaches as you please, you will never get a railroad by so doing.'

DIFFUSION BANDWAGONS

The growth of the railway networks of industrialized countries was a long process. In most cases it took around 100 years between the start of construction of the first line and the final completion of the network, which was achieved in almost all industrialized countries by the 1930s. Ever since, the length of the world's railway network has remained constant at around 1.3 million km, although the network in industrialized countries is contracting (due to the growth of successful competitors, such as road and air transport), whereas in developing and industrializing countries the growth of the railways continued into the 1960s and in some countries (e.g. China, Brazil, India or the USSR) still continues at present.

The absolute size of the railway network developed varied, of course, significantly from country to country. The United States constructed the largest network, with a maximum size attained in 1929 of over 482,000 km. In the United Kingdom the maximum network size was attained in 1928 with close to 33,000 km, and in France in 1933 with around 43,000 km. Thus, saturation in the expansion of the railway networks was attained almost simultaneously in the major industrialized countries by the early 1930s. However, both the spatial and the per capita railway density in individual countries differed widely: at the time of the maximum extension of railway lines, the spatial density (km of railways per km^2) varied from 4.3 (United States) to around 16 (United Kingdom). The per capita railway den-

48

sity (km of railways per 10,000 population) varies even more among indus-trialized countries: from around 5 (present-day USSR) to over 38 (the United States in the 1930s).

The diffusion of railways in industrial core countries and of basic trans-formations in railway technology took the form of an international diffusion bandwagon, with interconnected development trajectories related to their integration in terms of technology and capital transfers (see Table A1 in the Appendix).

For these reasons, the diffusion bandwagon patterns make it possible to identify countries with different growth trajectories (i.e. expansion of their railway networks even after the 1930s), which are apparently decoupled from the growth dynamics of the core countries during a particular eco-nomic expansion phase. The second expansion pulse of the USSR after 1930, as well as the continuing growth of railway networks in many deve-loping countries (i.e. their different diffusion trajectories) can be seen as a reflection of the fact that these countries were not integrated into the dynamics of economic growth and development of the industrial core coun-tries driving the post Second World War expansion of the world economy.

To summarize, in a particular development phase, growth proceeds in all core countries through a similar dynamic process, that is, in the form of an international diffusion bandwagon. Growth rates are not distributed uni-formly between different countries: early starters exhibit a slower dynamic than late-comers, and both display a synchronous pattern in the completion of a particular phase of development. The example of the expansion of the railway networks also underlines the critical importance of integration into technical knowledge, skills and capital flows for successful participation in a particular expansion bandwagon. This is all the more important for late-comers, if they are to catch up successfully with the core countries.

Heterogeneity in diffusion levels

A major observation that can be drawn from the analysis of the railway bandwagon example is heterogeneity among countries in the growth of the technological systems involved. In fact, as shown in Figure 2, the later a country started railway construction, the more diffusion levels appear to decrease.

Similar analyses suggest that this trend is not confined to the case of rail-ways. The implication is that, for developing countries, successful catching up will involve the acquisition of the technologies and infrastructures of the forthcoming development trajectory discussed above. Exaggeration some-times serves to illustrate a particular argument: imagine the validity of a long-term economic growth or development strategy which would have been defined with reference to achievements of industrialized countries around 1870, such as the length of canals and railways, the installed horse-power of steam engines, or Bessemer steel production (with an energy consumption more than ten times as high as present-day production), and which would have been suggested as a target for the industrialization and catching up of Japan in 1930!

Two main conclusions can be drawn with respect to the density levels resulting from the diffusion of large, pervasive infrastructure systems.

First, diffusion levels are different (heterogeneous) even within the core countries developing along a similar trajectory at various historical economic expansion periods, as a result of different boundary conditions prevailing in individual countries. It is therefore absolutely pointless to infer targets from the diffusion level achieved in early-starter countries (e.g. the United Kingdom for railways or the United States for automobiles) in order

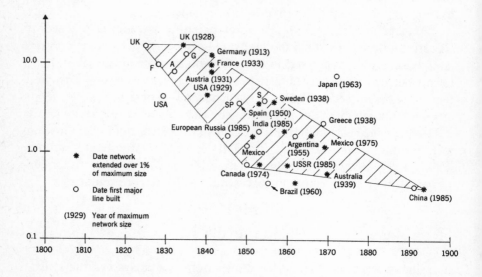

FIG. 2. Spatial railway density envelope versus network construction start-up date (km of railways per 100 km²). After Grübler, 1988.

This analysis focuses on the ultimate density levels achieved in countries that were not part of the 'railway bandwagon'. A number of developing countries continued railway construction after the saturation and contraction of railways in the industrialized core countries. However, the growth of railway networks in late follower countries did not occur to the same extent as in the core countries participating in the railway bandwagon. The indicator of diffusion levels which has been

50

to pursue them in other countries. Diffusion levels (network density) were very heterogeneous even among the countries forming the railway bandwagon, and the fact that in the United States the ultimate automobile density may approach one vehicle per inhabitant after the year 2000, does not imply that such a level is a realistic (or desirable) forecast for Austria or France, where densities below 0.5 vehicle per inhabitant appear to be typical for the ultimate automobile saturation level.

Heterogeneity is also a feature of the technological design and institutional embedding of infrastructures. Even if a similar functional structure, say in the transport sector, exists between different countries, this functional similarity may be achieved by different technological and/or organizational settings. For instance, a striking functional similarity exists between the long-distance passenger transport systems of the United States and the USSR. In both countries, the dominant long-distance passenger-transport mode is based on the internal-combustion engine and highway

---

chosen here is the railway density per km² (rather than per capita density, which diverges even more between industrialized and developing countries, owing to the considerable differential in population growth-rates). When considering the spatial railway densities resulting from the growth of these various 'railway late-comers', it turns out that the later a country started railway construction, the more the diffusion levels appear to decrease.

Two stages have been defined in the construction of national railway networks. First, the year the network extended for the first time over 1 per cent of its final maximum size, using either the historical dates indicated in Figure 2, or in cases such as China – where the network is still growing – the present density level. The second data point refers to the date the first railway line of national importance was constructed.

Figure 2 suggests that railway densities can be regrouped by a declining 'density envelope' as a function of the date when railway construction began. The later a country started, the smaller the proportion of railway lines it constructed. The only exception is Japan, where construction started rather late (in the 1870s), but achieved a network of a similar scale (density) as in the industrial core countries. This may indicate that Japan was developing its infrastructural endowment as early as in the second half of the nineteenth century to prepare its spectacular catching up which took place in the twentieth century.

As a similar analysis suggests, the conclusions drawn from Figure 2 are not confined to the case of railways, but also apply to the diffusion of more recent transport systems, in particular car ownership. Here again, diffusion levels of late-following countries do not reach those of the first countries to start motorization. If future development patterns in this case follow the railway precedent, we should not expect (private car) motorization in countries of the Second and Third Worlds at levels similar to those of industrialized countries.

infrastructure. In the case of the United States, however, transportation is achieved by (private) individual road vehicles, whereas in the USSR it is based on (collective) bus-transport operations. On the other hand, the trend towards public air transport, measured in terms of the increasing market share of air transport in total long-distance passenger kilometres, is similar in both countries.

The heterogeneity in diffusion levels, technological and institutional designs and embedding options becomes even greater when considering countries which are not among the core countries of a particular development phase. Returning to our example of the railway network densities, we observe that China would have to increase its present railway network by a factor of over twenty (!) in order to achieve a spatial railway density of the same order as that of the industrialized core countries in the 1930s. Not only is this highly unfeasible, it is simply absurd to suggest repeating the intensity levels of a growth trajectory of a development phase that has been superseded and is now of minor importance for further economic growth in industrialized countries. We contend that a similar statement also holds true for the massive diffusion of car ownership to levels similar to those that have been achieved in industrialized countries.

Heterogeneity is obviously even greater among developing countries. In fact, heterogeneity and social diversity have become inherent structural characteristics of developing countries, which are often (inappropriately) subsumed under a common heading. Thus, we suggest that traditional conceptualizations in terms of bi-polar models (North–South) may indeed be oversimplifications, especially when considering the initial conditions and catch-up possibilities in a new development phase, which are and will be extremely diverse among developing countries. This heterogeneity will need to be taken into account when defining criteria of sustainability of various development trajectories. Such criteria will ultimately have to be defined over a spatially heterogeneous system, consisting of clusters of interacting spatially related systems, which may not necessarily be in geographic proximity to each other.

Thus, any scenario of future development and catching up has to account for the different boundary conditions prevailing in different countries when assessing diffusion levels or even technological-choice options. As a result, (desirable) diffusion levels (e.g. infrastructure endowments) cannot be defined in a given country through a normative framework inferred from the diffusion levels achieved in another. Early starters may serve as a 'development model' only at very specific periods in time, that is, when catching up within a particular diffusion bandwagon characteristic of a given development phase, but not at later periods.

These considerations are obviously of great significance for developing countries, and the very nature of the transition to an emerging new development phase holds important implications for investment strategies and for anticipated resource consumption levels. When such a transition takes place, all indicators traditionally employed to describe 'appropriate' levels and trajectories of development (such as the example of railway densities or car-ownership rates discussed above) become progressively inadequate. For the same reason, Malthusian resource limits resulting from the extrapolation of indicators which may have seemed realistic under a previous growth regime (say per capita car ownership or oil consumption, steel intensity per unit of GNP, etc.), in fact become hypothetical, since they ignore the discontinuities of change and structural transition to new phases of development. Thus, the very concept of sustainability, especially when it entails economic development and technological change, has to be redefined as an evolutionary one. In the context of sustainable development, the rate of change of the structure of demand (i.e. the transition to a new development phase) may be a more serious limiting factor than absolute levels of demand and resulting strains on the resource base, which undergoes constant evolution through improvement in exploration (for example, the significant increase of the resource potential of natural gas discussed above), extraction, recycling and substitution technologies.

A long-term perspective on economic development thus leads us to emphasize, in particular, the discontinuous nature of technological, organizational and institutional innovations which become absorbed into our economies and societies. We appear to be engaged in a transition to a new phase of development, which will be quantitatively and qualitatively different in its final realization, with new technologies, infrastructures, skill levels, institutional and organizational settings as dominant driving forces that will shape the future structure of economies and their future trajectories.

We have tentatively sketched out some of the technological characteristics of the emerging new development phase in the area of energy (natural gas), transportation (air transportation) and manufacturing (micro-electronics). These represent only some of the major lines of development, singled out here because they seem to be the most determinant at present. Advances in other areas, ranging from biotechnology to supraconductivity – and including, for example, opto-electronics, bio-electronics and artificial intelligence – will probably contribute at least as much to shaping the overall characteristics of the new development phase. It may be anticipated that the major future driving forces will be more in the direction of enhancing qualitative characteristics in terms of efficiency, environmental quality, and system integration shaped by the philosophy of 'just-in-time' production, than in a repetition of the quantitative growth trajectory of energy- and material-intensive products and processes characteristic of the post Second World War development phase.

In the light of past history, we have stressed the importance of integration into international flows of capital and technological knowledge in order to make more effective use of the opportunities offered by the diffusion of a new socio-technological bandwagon involving a quantum leap in potential productivity of economies and offering a wide range of growth opportunities. This holds important implications for the development of appropriate financial and technological resource transfers to developing countries, especially in the areas which we have discussed as emerging as key technological elements of the new development period.

Once again, we must caution in this context against the prescriptive character of some development scenarios which do not account for heterogeneity in socio-technological options or in ultimate intensity (diffusion) levels. Heterogeneity has been, and will continue to be, one of the essential factors shaping the introduction of new technologies and their growth potential in developing countries.

References and bibliography

ARTHUR, B. 1988. Competing Technologies: An Overview. In: G. Dosi et al. (eds.), *Technical Change and Economic Theory*. London/New York, Pinter Publishers.

AUSUBEL, J. H.; SLADOVICH H. E. (eds.), 1989. *Technology and Environment*. Washington D.C., US National Academy of Engineering.

BROOKS, H. 1988. 'Some Propositions about Sustainability', Cambridge, Mass., Harvard University. (Unpublished draft.)

CEDIGAZ, 1985, 1987. *Natural Gas in the World*. Rueil-Malmaison, CEDIGAZ.

DOSI, G. 1983. Technological Paradigms and Technological Trajectories, The Determinants and Directions of Technical Change and the Transformation of the Economy. In: C. Freeman (ed.), *Long Waves in the World Economy*. London, Butterworth.

VAN DUIJN, J. J. 1983. *The Long Wave in Economic Life*. London, George Allen & Unwin.

FREEMAN, C. (ed.). 1983. *Long Waves in the World Economy*. London, Butterworth.

FREEMAN, C.; PEREZ, C. 1988. Structural Crises of Adjustment, Business Cycles and Investment Behaviour. In: G. Dosi et al. (eds.), *Technical Change and Economic Theory*. London/New York, Pinter Publishers.

GRÜBLER, A. 1988. *The Rise and Fall of Infrastructures: Dynamics of Evolution and Technological Change in Transport*. Vienna/Heidelberg, Technical University of Vienna/Physica Verlag.

GUILE, B.; BROOKS H. (eds.). 1987. *Technology and Global Industry, Companies and Nations in the World Economy*. Washington D.C., National Academy Press.

KONDRATIEFF, N. D. 1926. Die langen Wellen in der Konjunktur. *Archiv für Sozial-wissenschaft und Sozialpolitik,* Vol. 56, pp. 573–609.

MARCHETTI, C. 1985. Swings, Cycles and the Global Economy. *New Scientist,* No. 1454, pp. 12–15.

NAKICENOVIC, N. 1987. Patterns of Change: Technological Substitution and Long Waves in the United States. In: T. Vasko (ed.), *The Long Wave Debate.* Berlin/Heidelberg, Springer Verlag.

NOWOTNY, H. 1988. Long-term and Short-term Strategies for Science and Technology Policies in Developing Countries. Paper prepared for the Meeting of the International Council for Science Policy Studies, Paris, 24–25 March, 1988. University of Vienna.

OECD, 1979. *Interfutures: Facing the Future, Mastering the Probable and Managing the Unpredictable.* Paris, OECD.

PEREZ, C. 1983. Structural Change and the Assimilation of New Technologies in the Economic and Social System. *Futures,* Vol. 15, No. 4, pp. 357–75.

PEREZ, C.; SOETE, L. 1988. Catching up in Technology: Entry Barriers and Windows of Opportunity. In: G. Dosi et al. (eds.), *Technical Change and Economic Theory.* London/New York, Pinter Publishers.

ROSTOW, W. W. 1960. *The Process of Economic Growth,* 2nd ed. New York, W. W. Norton.

SCHUMPETER, J. A. 1935. The Analysis of Economic Change. *Review of Economic Statistics.* Vol. 17, pp. 2–10.

——. 1939. *Business Cycles, a Theoretical, Historical and Statistical Analysis of the Capitalist Process,* Vols. I and II. New York, McGraw-Hill.

US NATIONAL ACADEMY OF ENGINEERING. 1988. *The Technological Dimensions of International Competitiveness.* Washington D.C., USNAE.

WILLIAMS, R. H.; LARSON, E. D.; ROSS M. H. 1987. Materials, Affluence, and Industrial Energy Use. *Annual Review of Energy,* Vol. 12, pp. 99–144.

3. The diverse futures of developing countries

A long-standing view of the world quartered by East–West and North–South confrontations is now rapidly changing, giving way to a new perception of ongoing shifts and realignments. Eastern countries are facing up in a variety of ways to the challenge of profound structural adaptations. In the West, major developments include the creation of a unified market in Western Europe, accompanied by a new complex pattern of international trade agreements (for example, between the United States and Canada, or between the United States and Japan), and the emergence of a sense of common interest among countries in different regions, such as the Pacific. All these developments bear witness to changing patterns of international competition and, ultimately, of political and economic relations. Among countries of the South, the heterogeneity of situations generates major differences in strategies and approaches. For example:

The very poor countries with limited natural resources and industrialization prospects, whose immediate future essentially depends on agricultural advances and on their absorptive capacity for external aid. The larger ones will have a broader range of options to formulate their own strategies.

The giants, such as China and India, which suffer from enormous regional disparities that call for diversified policies.

Countries whose natural resources exports affect growth prospects positively – or negatively, when a national economy turns out to be locked in the position of an exporter of raw materials.

Countries that are increasingly industrialized and as such have become significant actors in the international redistribution of economic activities, but are faced with unprecedented challenges resulting from the emergence of new factors of economic growth.

Countries that have industrialized to a fuller extent – the newly industrialized countries (NICs) – and which must face up to the difficulty of achieving balanced national development while maintaining their competitive stance in a context of fierce international competition in number of key areas.

This overall diversity will naturally be reflected by the great variety of approaches and goals pursued by the development policies of different countries. This being said, it remains that all countries are confronted alike with the same political, economic and social world context which must be taken into account to determine future courses of action. Five major driving forces now at work will in particular play a major part in designing the future of all countries:

1. In the strategic sphere, the fact that the two superpowers have begun a process of arms reduction and commitments which would bring military efforts more in line with their economic feasibility. The outcome is still uncertain: renewed efforts to modernize armed forces according to new priorities, or shifts of emphasis in the allocation of resources to respond to social and economic problems and thus strengthen national competitiveness.

2. In the political sphere, the emergence of diverse political aspirations (in particular at regional level), and a new willingness, in many regions, to look for peaceful solutions to conflicts in the face of ample evidence of the limits of coercion.

3. In the international sphere, a process of globalization of national economies, enhanced by new worldwide communications infrastructures, characterized by the internationalization of financial markets, massive and rapid capital movements, and the emergence of transnational actors which cannot be controlled by a single government and have direct access to capital, skills, know-how and markets.

4. In the technological sphere, the emergence of 'hi-tech' in areas as diverse as information, communications, materials, biotechnology, etc. These advanced technologies have generated, and will continue to generate, new economic activities in industries and services, while their diffusion throughout the industrial fabric entails radical changes in production, modes of production and the nature of products. As a result, the world may be entering a new cycle of growth based on access to and mastery of these new technologies.

5. In the environmental sphere, global changes seem to threaten the earth's physical, chemical and climatic systems, with possibly catastrophic effects on world agriculture and, more generally, on inhabitable areas in all continents (e.g. as a result of rising sea-levels). Provision against these threats is inconceivable without international action. The issue is closely linked to that of development: the production of CO_2 increases with traditional processes of industrialization, and poverty is at the root of behaviour patterns such as the burning of forests.

All these factors will determine national options for all countries in years to come. They will, in particular, play a major role in shaping the international environment in which developing countries will search for a way to grow.

Their ability to cope with these challenges at home, and to contribute to the development of international policies, will obviously be a direct function of their past achievements on a development trajectory. It would seem, therefore, of the utmost importance to obtain an overall assessment of their accomplishments in this respect.

However, there are no adequate comprehensive indicators of development which can reflect the complex cultural, social, economic and political factors at play when the concept of 'development' is considered with all its multi-dimensional implications. At best, there are some indicators of the penetration of Western patterns into different societies.

It remains that the evolution of each society must be seen in its own context, as an organic process undergoing continuous transformation. In various social and cultural environments, Western inputs combine with others. The diversity of these interactions reflects the world's heterogeneity, which is one of its most powerful sources of creativity. Thus, in spite of the powerful homogenizing forces at play today throughout the world, not the least of which is technology, the challenge of development is to open a way for each culture to preserve its individuality and define its own approach to new challenges and opportunities.

Science and technology (S&T) will play essential roles: science because it offers a method and a process to establish new truths and to challenge accepted truths, and because it has come to be intimately linked to technology, which holds the key to the satisfaction of human needs on a large scale. However, science and technology can only take root in a given society if their structures and goals are well matched to prevailing modes of thinking and of doing, in particular to local traditional technologies. Thus, while it is clear that any process of development will seek to satisfy human dignity and material needs, the means to do so will not necessarily – and in most cases could not – follow the same path that has been followed historically by the industrialized nations.

Science and technology cannot be imported ready-made because they do not fill a void. Provision of opportunities for study abroad, investments, networks and alliances with foreign academic and industrial research teams, import of capital goods, acquisition of patents and hiring of consultants – all these mechanisms provide means by which foreign S&T can complement pre-existing national approaches. But their full contribution is narrowly dependent on the extent to which they can be embedded into existing social structures and blended with prevailing traditions and cultures.

For these reasons, there are no indicators of development which could reflect this 'embedding' and this 'blending' to account, for example, for the evolution of traditional technologies. Hence the first difficulty in attempting to sketch a 'typology' of the developing world.

A second difficulty is due to the fact that scientific and technological resources (in terms of trained people and specialized institutions) do not suffice. Research activities, the quest for solutions to economic and social problems, and the successful implementation of these solutions, imply continuity of purpose and the existence of a socio-cultural environment which promotes exchanges of views and opinions as well as the persistent pursuit of activities on a long-term basis. The scientific and technological potential of a given country is thus affected by various aspects such as cultural traditions, the extent of civil rights and political participation, electoral patterns and the diffusion of democratic attitudes throughout society. The typology suggested below is not sufficient on this account, since it focuses on economic capacity, educational achievements and scientific and technological resources in the strict sense. It should be interpreted in this light, knowing that many of the crucial factors which affect a society's ability to take advantage of modern science – and which would call for the design of a broad and structured base for the evaluation of a country's development – have not been taken into account.

A third difficulty is related to the specific concern of this report – namely the creation, exploitation and management of the S&T base. What is essentially at stake here is the ability of a given society to take advantage of the opportunities offered by such a base – in other words to exploit it. Yet there are no adequate indicators of the output of research and development. Those which are most commonly used in industrialized countries (such as indicators of techno-scientific infrastructure, rates of publication and scientific citation statistics, patents or licences) are highly controversial and their interpretation is very uncertain. A further difficulty is the lack of uniform and recent data on some of the basic structural features of the economy, the educational system and S&T activities in developing countries.

This being said, and in spite of all these drastic limitations, it is necessary to have a better understanding of the relative situation of countries in constructing their own S&T bases in order to design national strategies for development which will be based on informed consideration of specific national and regional contexts. This chapter will essentially suggest a typology based on the creation of an S&T base, after taking stock of efforts already made to develop other typologies based on industrial and economic accomplishments.

Chapter 2 suggested the possibility of producing more elaborate and technology-based typologies – for example, by bringing to light the relative place of countries with respect to different technological bandwagons. More complex methodologies can and should be developed in this respect, with emphasis on the production of longitudinal analyses which will make it possible to identify and monitor development trajectories over time.

This kind of effort, however, is at present seriously hampered by the lack of homogeneous data on most countries. The information used here is very incomplete and heterogeneous – but it does exist. The use that has been made of it in no way implies that we hold to the notion of a linear development chain, which would automatically lead from the creation of S&T resources to the expansion of industrial activities.

Typologies based on economic accomplishments

One method of classification is based upon the share of manufacturing value added (MVA) in the gross domestic product (GDP) of a country. Using this method, countries can be divided into industrialized countries, semi-industrialized countries, industrialized and non-industrial. The last three would constitute basic categories for a typology of developing countries.

But this approach is open to criticism. First, there is no automatic rise in per capita income as a result of a rise in the share of MVA. Second, service industries should also be taken into account. Third, the expansion of the manufacturing sector in developing countries is not necessarily linked at all stages with the successful exploitation of a national S&T base, but may be due to benefits drawn from other competitive advantages.

Other, composite, indicators have been used by various organizations such as the World Bank and the United Nations Commission for Trade and Development (UNCTAD). These typologies include, for example, average growth-rate of GDP, average per capita income, industrial output, capital formation, skill formation at different levels, growth-rates of heavy and capital-goods industries, growth of exports and imports and the share of manufactured goods in imports and exports, etc. These typologies produce groupings such as 'low-income countries', 'middle-income countries', 'higher-income countries'. They provide an indication of economic accomplishments but, once again, no clear picture of the creation and exploitation of an S&T base.

Another approach has been followed by the Ameritrust and SRI International, which have devised indicators of economic capacity to measure the long-term economic potential of nine regions (fifty countries). The model has also been applied to analyse the potential of S&T for economic development at Karnataka in India. Indicators are grouped under three different headings: accessible technology (for example, research articles per faculty, science and engineering graduates, R&D in universities and industry, number of patents issued, etc.); skilled and adaptable labour force; and capital availability. This approach obviously comes a step closer to a typology based on actual S&T capabilities. In addition to the fact that some redefinition of indicators is needed to account for the specific context of developing countries, a major difficulty is that the data is very patchy in many of these areas and does not provide an up-to-date comprehensive picture.

Finally, we could conceive of a typology that would focus on policies, bringing to light the major facets of government priorities directed at S&T and grouping countries according to the prime rationale of these policies. Major goals might include, for example: absence of any explicit policy intent linked to S&T, response to external challenge, modernization of the economy, strengthening economic development, safeguarding the environment, training S&T personnel, technology transfer, the promotion of basic science, and so on.

Such a policy-oriented approach to a typology of science and technology policies might shed some light on the level at which S&T-related priorities are established by different groups of countries. But it remains an obviously crude instrument which may not be much more, in the final analysis, than a classification of declarations of intent rather than a reflection of reality.

Typologies reflecting the creation of an S&T base

The design of an S&T-related typology proposed here will reflect the relative size of countries, their income, their R&D intensity and their S&T human resources, as well as their accomplishments at third-level education. On this basis, an aggregate typology of S&T capabilities will be suggested. This typology is assessed in light of economic accomplishments in the manufacturing sector.

THE DISTRIBUTION OF OVERALL HUMAN RESOURCES

Population is obviously an essential determinant of the nature of the S&T base and of the ways in which it can be established. Small countries cannot have the same aspirations as larger countries, in this respect, and the possibilities open to very large countries are still greater: in the latter, a very small percentage of the population engaged in scientific and technological activities may turn out to constitute a sizeable cohort; in the former, a high percentage of scientific and technological personnel may often amount to only a hundred or so individuals. As a result, very small countries may find it difficult – if not impossible – to create even one university covering all fields of knowledge and delivering the whole hierarchy of degrees. These barriers will obviously provide special incentives for efforts to associate the population at large with the development effort (e.g. through increased participation of women), or to seek to achieve collective efficiencies through international co-operation and regional economic integration.

A distribution of countries according to population is shown in Table A1.[1] Countries have been grouped in six categories: (a) very very small; (b) very small; (c) small; (d) medium-sized; (e) large; and (f) very large. All it is possible to say at this stage is that the range is enormous and that, for the smaller countries, as noted above, it may turn out to be more difficult to establish an adequate S&T base. Difficult, but by no means impossible, as will be shown below.

THE DISTRIBUTION OF INCOME LEVELS

A classification of income levels in terms of per capita GDP is shown in Table A2. Four groupings are proposed, ranging from low-income countries to upper-income countries.

The higher the income, the easier it should be to establish an S&T base – and, presumably, the more ground may already have been covered in this direction. But aggregate statistics do not reflect actual distribution patterns of income within a society, which affect savings and productive investments: drastic inequalities in income distribution are obviously not conducive to widespread demands for a scientific and technological infrastructure. With these important reservations in mind, data on average per capita income nevertheless provide an aggregate indication of the various levels of theoretical ability to mobilize resources for science.

This general picture can be made more precise if we take into account other parameters, such as the exploitation of a commodity for exports and the importance of exports of manufactured products, and if we relate income level to size of population.

The countries which export more than 0.5 per cent of total world exports of a commodity have been underlined in Table A2. Predictably, the number of such countries increases as one goes up the scale. In any case, the availability of such commodities should have a favourable effect on the ability to establish a technology base.

The share of developing countries in world exports of manufactured products, shown in Table A3, singles out seven countries – the newly

1. Tables A1 to A15 will be found in the Appendix.

63

industrialized countries, which account for almost 90 per cent of the total manufactured exports of developing countries. Here again, special situations exist for the development and management of the S&T base.

There is no correlation between size and income level. In other words, as illustrated in Table A4, some of the smaller countries have achieved some of the highest per capita income levels. The cases of the Bahamas, Iceland and Luxembourg – among the non-oil-producing smaller countries – are especially relevant: their success has been achieved by taking advantage of geographic location or by the establishment of a highly specialized S&T base, as in the case of Iceland. The challenge is greater, but the creation of a broad base is impossible. Size, measured in absolute terms, is not an adequate indicator of the prospects for development of an S&T base.

RESEARCH AND DEVELOPMENT INTENSITY

There are fewer countries which provide data on their R&D efforts, as summarized in Table A5. The availability of such data is, in itself, a probable indication of the policy relevance and importance attached to it.

Groups of countries have been defined according to their 'R&D intensity', assessed in terms of the R&D share of gross national product (GNP). Most developing countries belong to the first three groups, ranging from 0 to 0.9 per cent of GNP. It can be assumed that, above 0.4 per cent, a domestic S&T resource exists, which should be carefully managed and exploited to serve national development targets.

Another approach, in terms of the share of R&D scientists and engineers in the population, is suggested in Table A6, which stresses the diversity of situations. Countries which achieve a higher ranking in this table than in Table A5 seem to suffer from insufficient concentration of R&D resources, which is not a factor of effectiveness.

Finally, Table A7 focuses on the importance of research in the higher education sector, where it is a decisive element in the training of future generations of scientists, and in providing a 'seed-corn', through basic research, for the development of national capabilities. Data on this type of research unfortunately cover only a relatively small number of countries.

ACCOMPLISHMENTS IN S&T EDUCATION

The diffusion of an awareness of science and technology is a fundamental condition for their successful social integration. An indication of this degree of awareness can be brought to light by showing the extent to which members of the general public have been trained in science and in tech-

64

nology. This can be measured in absolute numbers, as in Table A9, which refers to the number of potential scientists and engineers in a given population.

A given country may have a large number of scientists and engineers, yet this may represent only a small percentage of the population. These scientists will presumably be concentrated in urban areas and relatively isolated from the rest of the population. Conversely, a country may have only a small group of people educated in S&T, but they may represent a larger share of the population.

These two situations offer very different challenges for the management of the S&T base and its effective exploitation. This picture would not be complete, however, without an indication of the future potential, represented by the number of third-level students relative to the population, shown in Table A8. These students are national assets, and groupings of countries illustrate their relative advantages or handicaps for the future of the S&T base.

Finally, Table A10 distributes countries according to the relative importance of the scientific and technological workforce directly employed in R&D by industry, a factor that is obviously essential in the design of future development projects and in order to benefit from international cooperative efforts. Although this type of data unfortunately does not distinguish employment by subsidiaries of foreign firms from employment by national industries, it does provide a significant indicator of the extent to which scientific and technological resources are harnessed to industry nationally. This indicator might be further refined by bringing to light the number of women in the S&T workforce, thus reflecting progress accomplished in capitalizing on the national potential.

AN OVERALL TYPOLOGY OF S&T CAPABILITIES

The most relevant indicators of S&T capabilities are thus shown in Tables A2 to A10. They can be combined to achieve a 'scoreboard' according to the groups achieved by countries in each case.[1] A cautionary note is

1. The scoreboard has been developed in the following way. Countries included in Tables A2 to A10 have been ranked in four groups (I to IV) according to their achievements in each case. The marks gathered by each country have been added (for example, a country that would have achieved the lowest grouping (I) in each of the nine tables, would rate 9. A country with the highest possible marks would rate 36. Countries missing from at most two tables (data not available) would be rated zero (0) in these tables, under the assumption that lack of data would reflect at least lack of interest in achievements in this area, or very low achievement. Countries would thus be distributed among four groups (A to D) according to their total marks. A final check was conducted to eliminate glaring discrepancies, essentially due to absent or

obviously needed at this stage: a scoreboard of this type has many limitations, especially when drawing on different indicators of different things. In particular, when some indicators overlap, the scoreboard may well turn out to be more or less misleading.

This implies that the scoreboard should not be taken too literally in assessing the ranking of a given country. As noted above, many efforts are still needed to produce the kind of comprehensive and structured data base that will make it possible to establish a reliable typology. What matters here, however, is the overall pattern which makes it possible to attribute certain basic common characters to certain groups of countries.

The result is illustrated in Table 2, where four groups of countries have been identified: Group A – no S&T base; Group B – fundamental elements of an S&T base; Group C – S&T base established; Group D – industrialized countries with effective S&T bases, which are outside the scope of the present report. In order to account for the particular features of some countries, the table identifies those which are exporters of commodities and, separately, OPEC countries.

TABLE 2. Distribution of S&T capabilities

Country	Exporter of commodities	OPEC member
Group A		
Benin		
Bhutan		
Burkina Faso		
Cape Verde		
Chad		
Comoros		
Ethiopia		
Guinea-Bissau		
Haiti	Lao People's Dem. Rep.	
Lesotho		
Mali		
Mozambique		
Namibia		
Nepal		
Sao Tomé and Principe		
Sierra Leone		
Timor		
Uganda	Zaire	

---

inaccurate data, for example, when a country would have been inserted in Group A because of its low overall rating, in spite of a high level of industrial and/or academic activities.

Country	Exporter of commodities	OPEC member
Albania		
Angola		
Myanmar		
Cameroon		
Central African Rep.		
Djibouti		
Equatorial Guinea		
Grenada	Liberia	
Madagascar		
Maldives		
Niger		
Somalia		
Suriname		
Yemen	Zimbabwe	
Bahamas		
Belize		
Bangladesh		
Botswana		
Burundi		
Dominica		
Guyana		
Haiti	Honduras	
Mauritania	Oman	
Solomon Islands	Papua New Guinea	
Swaziland		

Group B

Brunei-Darussalam		Algeria
Cambodia		
Fiji		
Gabon	Ghana	
Jamaica	Kenya	
Dem. People's Rep. of Korea		
Mongolia	Nigeria	
Romania		
Rwanda	Togo	
Tunisia		
Afghanistan	Bolivia	
	China	
	Cyprus	Iraq
Malawi	United Arab Emirates	
	Zambia	
	Bahrain	
Barbados		

67

TABLE 2 – *continued*

Country	Exporter of commodities	OPEC member
Dominican Republic		
Guinea	Malaysia	Indonesia
		Islamic Rep. of Iran
Malta		
Paraguay	Senegal	Saudi Arabia
	Sri Lanka	
Syrian Arab Republic		

Group C

Country	Exporter of commodities	OPEC member
	Colombia	
	Sudan	
	Thailand	
Uruguay	Costa Rica	
Guatemala		
Guyana		
Hong Kong	Jordan	
Lebanon		
Nicaragua		
Seychelles		
Mauritius	Pakistan	
Panama	India	
	Viet Nam	
Congo	Philippines	Libyan Arab Jamahiriya
	Chile	
	Mexico	Qatar
	Ecuador	
Samoa	El Salvador	
Greece		
Portugal		
Trinidad and Tobago		
Turkey		
Finland	Argentina	
	Egypt	
	Peru	Kuwait
	Brazil	
	Cuba	Venezuela
Israel	Iceland	
Republic of Korea		
New Zealand		
Singapore		

Group D

Country	Exporter of commodities	OPEC member
Poland		
Sweden		

Country	Exporter of commodities	OPEC member
USSR		
Yugoslavia		
Austria		
Belgium		
Bulgaria		
Canada		
Hungary		
Spain		
United Kingdom		
Czechoslovakia		
Ireland		
Australia		
Denmark		
Italy		
Norway		
Switzerland		
France		
Germany		
Japan		
Netherlands		
United States		

Two special cases are, however, virtually unclassifiable and call for a special group. China and India both have low per capita GDP, but they are distinguished by their large populations and large territorial size. Both have experience of planning systems, and the industrial and manufacturing sectors have a large share in the structure of production. They have high S&T manpower potential in absolute terms due to their huge populations, but low in terms of percentage of the total population. In such countries, the integration of S&T capabilities raises a number of problems, which are obviously different from those of other countries, including the industrialized ones. The scale on which problems must be identified and tackled bears little resemblance to other countries' experiences, which may thus be of little relevance. The challenge here is thus to create radically new conditions for the effective development and exploitation of the S&T base.

This distribution of developing countries into Groups A, B and C will be taken as a reference point for subsequent observations in this book. It should be kept in mind, however, that such a classification can only be approximate: data is lacking for many countries which have not been included and, when available, the data is not always as reliable as one might wish.

In addition, the grouping of countries according to S&T capabilities is not directly related to economic performance. This point is illustrated by Table A11, which ranks countries according to the percentage of the manufacturing sector in GDP, and mentions the grouping achieved by each country in Table 2. It can be seen that, while many countries in Group A rank low in the new table, significant discrepancies do occur. These may be due to erroneous data, but also to the fact that the growth of the manufacturing sector in many developing countries has not yet been directly linked with the availability of S&T resources. The situation in this respect may be fundamentally altered in future years, as will be seen in Chapter 4: the new conditions for growth are increasingly linked to the ability to manage and exploit new technological opportunities.

Another drawback of the typology proposed above is that it is a static one, reflecting the situation of each country at a given point in time. It conveys no sense of movement, a movement which is inherent to the development process. And it does not reflect setbacks and fluctuations which have affected many countries in the recent past as a consequence of the international crisis of the last decade. The following section will attempt to account for these fluctuations.

The limitations of a static typology

Recent years have witnessed major shifts and fluctuations in the patterns of development of many countries. Since the mid 1970s, economic difficulties have struck at the heart of the development process, as shown in Table A12, which illustrates the average growth-rates of MVA for certain countries from 1980 to 1986. A number of countries in all three groups have experienced negative growth. The implications must have been drastic for the S&T resources of the countries in question: not only has momentum not been preserved, but what had been achieved may have been severely compromised by budgetary cutbacks and premature interruption of long-standing efforts.

Table A12 also illustrates the fact that, when taken in a dynamic perspective, the groups cannot be used to forecast patterns of national development. Three countries which have achieved the most substantial rates of progress belong respectively to Group A (Lesotho), Group B (China) and Group C (Republic of Korea). Conversely, the countries that have experienced negative growth belong to all three groups of developing countries.

The lessons are clear: science and technology have not been sufficient conditions for continued industrial development (some countries with obvious S&T capabilities have suffered disproportionately from the economic crisis), and have not been necessary conditions either (some countries with very small or non-existent S&T bases have fared relatively well). In other words, S&T capabilities, where they existed, have not proved able to assist against the impact of the economic recession. Basic technical competence and trading abilities may have turned out, in several cases, to be better assets for the initial growth of the manufacturing sectors.

This, as noted above, may not always be the case in future, in view of the prospective importance of new technologies and of the need to consolidate past achievements on a more sophisticated structural base. But these considerations stress the importance of the socio-economic underpinnings of the effective exploitation of S&T bases: a sound educational base, coupled with third-level technical and vocational training well designed to meet local requirements.

In these areas, possible discontinuities and fluctuations may have enormous long-term negative effects. Table A13 illustrates the fact that this is by no means a theoretical consideration. This table shows the prportion of GNP devoted to third-level education between 1975 and 1986 by a number of countries. For many countries, drops in the magnitude of efforts were significant at the beginning of the decade. This affects countries belonging to all groups, as brought to light in Table A14, which shows the ranking achieved by each of the countries at the beginning and at the end of the period (countries for which data was only available for one of these dates have been ranked correspondingly but are not shown). According to this table: out of eleven countries in Group A, five lost rank; out of fourteen countries in Group B, three lost rank; out of fifteen countries in Group C, eight lost rank; both countries in Group D (mentioned as examples of this group) lost rank. Three observations are called for here.

First, the higher the level of past accomplishments, the more vulnerable the educational system seems to be to economic fluctuations. This underlines the vulnerability of S&T bases in developing countries and the need to establish safeguards against the disastrous impact of decisions which may instantaneously reduce to nothing the efforts of many years.

Second, efforts to invest in third-level education are relatively higher in Group A countries than those in other groups. This certainly reflects the implementation of policies that allocate scarce resources to what is considered to have decisive importance for the future. However, there is little doubt that, in absolute terms, these efforts are often not sufficient. Given the relative share of resources already allocated by the countries in question, it seems obvious that additional support will usually not become available in the short term unless it comes from foreign sources.

Third, the typology of developing countries could be unstable. S&T bases may confer comparative advantages to a given country in world competition, but comparative advantages are not acquired once and for all.

They constitute volatile constellations of factors which can rapidly migrate from one country to another. In view of the fluctuations just brought to light, it is impossible not to fear that recent data may, when it becomes available, justify reallocation of countries among the three groups.

Alternative futures

It is with all these qualifications and misgivings that this section will refer to the three groups of developing countries that have been identified.

GROUP A: COUNTRIES WITH NO S&T BASE

These countries and regions are still in the initial stage of development with low per capita GDP, low S&T manpower potential and low percentage of industrial and manufacturing sectors in production. This group includes most African countries.

The main common feature of Group A, from the present perspective, is thus the lack of a scientific and technological infrastructure in education and research. But this weakness is rooted in an extremely fragile economic base characterized by the fledgling manufacturing sector, severe difficulties in agriculture, non-existent or unexploited natural resources, and general conditions of extreme poverty where basic food requirements are not met for a large proportion of the population, close to 90 per cent in many cases. The per capita income is extremely low and even if it doubles in the next decade it will still be extremely low.

The factors that perpetuate this situation may to some extent be directly related to harsh natural conditions and the unavailability of natural resources which could provide a starting-base for development. But in most cases, social and political characteristics (very high population, severe inequalities in income distribution, which is one of the causes of the insufficient creation of new wealth, weakness of the system for targeting resources) are at the core of the inability to generate dynamic economic processes. The long-standing deficiency of provisions made for education and training are simultaneously a cause and a consequence of this situation.

As a result, the impact of international exchanges and transfers – if their pattern does not change drastically to take account of basic structural needs – will continue to be of only limited significance for the solution of long-term development problems. Yet, in all cases, apart from the subsistence economy, economic activity is largely outward-oriented and dependent on other countries – in terms of trade or the import of capital, know-how or management capabilities. These international exchanges affect only small minorities within countries, leaving the majority only marginally concerned.

Furthermore, prospects for intraregional co-operation are often bleak, limited by historical antagonisms inherited from the past. Hence the major problems confronting development policies in these countries are as follows:

Political authorities do not have sufficient roots in the rural areas (where over 90 per cent of the population often live), are unable to demonstrate the benefits to be drawn from technological solutions, to promote the modernization of agricultural activities throughout the country and, more generally, to mobilize resources around a few priorities. As a result, modern agricultural 'islands' coexist with less productive traditional exploitations which do not benefit from investments, related services, and infrastructures.

Economic activity is dominated by agriculture and mining and, to a lesser degree, by a relatively overgrown service sector with strong bureaucratic overtones.

Industrialization is hampered by difficult structural obstacles linked to the decline of traditional activities, but there are few policies or guidelines for national or foreign investments. While identified natural resources are often relatively abundant, they remain virtually untapped. Industry employs only a small proportion of the labour force and must contend with the scarcity of local skilled staff.

Investments are essentially of foreign origin, and in most cases there are no effective counterweights to foreign influence. But it has become clear that industrial projects conceived abroad will not suffice to solve national problems; neither will national savings, since they grow very slowly – if at all.

The distribution of food aid, while absolutely necessary in many cases, fails to reach some of the potential recipients. In addition, it is often distributed in a manner that discourages national production.

These salient characteristics underline the social and political nature of many of the long-term development problems of the countries concerned, and the inadequacy of conventional or long-standing approaches.

This being said, however, there are enormous differences between countries in this group, which includes, for example, Asian countries (such as Bangladesh) with very large, dense populations, and countries (mainly in sub-Saharan Africa) with small populations occupying relatively large territories. In spite of the differences, the main challenges are very similar. What is at stake in all countries is to generate a virtuous circle of development that will not exclude access to the opportunities characteristic of the new phase of growth that industrialized countries have entered. In general, this calls for strong assertion of national priorities and a long-term effort to build the kind of solid base that will keep options open in these areas.

The future depends to a large extent on the availability of exploitable resources, in particular if industrialization is to rely largely on foreign initiatives, which will presumably concentrate on countries with abundant natural, mineral, agricultural and energy resources, and which can attract international capital by providing a 'suitable' investment climate. The two main avenues of industrial expansion will continue to be mineral processing and light manufacturing, essentially oriented to exports, since prospects for the development of domestic markets remain limited. In this context, three types of evolution are possible:

1. *The present situation of virtual economic stagnation, particularly with regard to agriculture, could continue for a long time in some countries and/or regions, often with fluctuations between famines and better years, giving rise to periods of political instability.*

2. *Increased foreign impetus given to economic growth with more intensive exploitation of national resources opening the way for industrialization and exports. However, more rapid growth would be entirely dependent on foreign initiatives and might well benefit only a local minority. Furthermore, one cannot expect these investments to encourage the overall development of national capabilities (in terms of manufacturing, management and service-delivery capabilities) related to the new technologies emerging in industrialized countries.*

3. *Endogenous development, giving priority to domestic requirements over demands by the world economy. This raises many problems of design and implementation (definition of priorities, mobilization of resources, organization of trade). It entails, in particular, a long-term effort for the creation of a strong and reliable pool of personnel trained in a vast number of key areas, ranging from administration and management to the provision of basic scientific and technological services, and including – most important of all – qualified and motivated teachers at all levels.*

GROUP B: COUNTRIES WITH FUNDAMENTAL ELEMENTS OF AN S&T BASE

These countries and regions are still in the process of industrialization. They have established a certain industrial basis, with moderate GDP per capita (upper- middle income and lower-middle income countries). Some have a relatively high percentage of potential S&T manpower, but the potential is low in absolute terms. This group includes Ghana, Indonesia, etc.

Group B, therefore, includes countries that have some elements of a basic S&T infrastructure. They are, by and large, mainly agricultural and exporters of raw materials, but have begun a process of industrialization. It includes countries of various sizes and socio-political structures, ranging from East Asia to the Middle East and North Africa.

Almost all these countries face the common challenge of capitalizing on past achievements to generate a new process of growth. In general, past policies have focused on investment (mostly foreign) into promising industrial ventures. Little attention has been paid to domestic economic problems and the requirements of a very large share of the population – requirements that have often become more and more explicit as a result of cultural changes and demands for redistribution of the benefits of economic expansion. At the same time, the limitations of the domestic markets represent an obstacle to the further growth of import-substitution industries.

Three factors contribute to this weakness of domestic markets: the export industry, based on processing of agricultural and/or mining products, has created few jobs; the manufacturing industry in the larger countries (e.g. Indonesia) has been aimed at import substitution with a low level of value added which has had a limited impact on domestic income and market growth; and there have been limited efforts to capitalize on traditional craft activities.

As a result, most of the countries in this group often face serious imbalances. On the one hand, between sectors of the economy, when the focus of development policies has been on the exploitation of natural resources, accompanied by insufficient agricultural growth, multiplication of speculative activities, rapid extension of the tertiary sector, and rising unemployment as a result of the capital-intensive nature of many new industrial ventures. On the other hand, in the social and cultural spheres, with conflicts between traditional and emerging (or imported) values, social groups with different stakes in the acceleration or deceleration of growth, and mounting pressures from the unemployed, the rural population and diverse minorities.

The future will obviously depend on the ability of the countries concerned to develop policies that will achieve some internal stability by a combination of better income distribution, provision of collective services in tune with the demands of the population, and more effective resource utilization. One significant asset in this direction relates to the fact that regional co-operation offers many diverse and attractive prospects, owing to the complementarity of national economies (in terms of the range of available resources, including human resources) in regions such as the Middle East, North Africa or East Asia. These potential advantages remain largely untapped at present, but in future the world trend towards regional groupings may also positively affect the regions concerned here.

75

Regional co-operation may be one of the most effective ways to construct rapidly a better S&T base, which needs to be extended, diversified, and mobilized for development purposes. This calls for a reinforcement of education and training as well as careful investment in research and development. The major alternative future courses include:

1. *De-industrialization, as a result of mismanagement and waste in the exploitation of dwindling natural resources, and of strategic choices that do not reflect the new trends on world markets, coupled with major domestic disruptions caused by conflicting social and cultural demands.*

2. *Fairly rapid aggregate growth based on natural resources, with the persistence of severe poverty problems for a large part of the population, and a resulting inability to enter a new period of expansion based on the development and diversification of the domestic demand.*

3. *Growth based on a combination of export-oriented industrialization and structural development of domestic activities, spearheaded by agricultural productivity gains and the provision of effective services that will open new opportunities for the introduction and diffusion of new technologies, and the creation of employment.*

GROUP C: COUNTRIES WITH AN ESTABLISHED S&T BASE

The countries and regions in this group have established an industrial basis, with a higher percentage of potential S&T manpower and relatively high per capita GDP. They include countries as diverse as Egypt, a large number of Latin American countries and the smaller Asian NICs as well as some of the largest Asian countries, such as India and Pakistan.

Like the previous groups, this one is highly heterogeneous. The larger the country concerned (as in the case of India or Pakistan), the more difficult it is to achieve balanced development, and poverty then remains a basic problem affecting large sectors of the population. The more so since, in most cases, population growth-rates remain high and social structures inegalitarian. Hence the threat of 'blocked societies', which – owing to a social stalemate between antagonistic forces – fail to generate the dynamics of change.

In many cases, industrialization faces a long-standing strategic dilemma: import-substitution policies will involve protectionism and excessive costs, and may delay the growth of competitive industry, but export-oriented strategies will often involve reliance on transnational corporations and consequent loss of control by governments accompanied by growth at the expense of domestic entrepreneurs.

These developments have often been accompanied (in particular in

76

Latin America) by growing structural balance of payment deficits and a related problem of growing indebtedness, which further limit the options available to the countries concerned.

Overall, however, the major past achievements of countries in this group have in some cases been based on massive industrialization and promotion of heavy industry, in others on an active strategy of export promotion based on careful assessment of market opportunities and prospects, provision of support to exporting candidates, and deliberate policies to attract external resources on very soft terms.

In addition, increasing attention has been devoted to food production and small industries. Skilled labour has generally been available at low wage levels, as a result of past massive investment in education and training.

Future development prospects may, however, be threatened by a number of structural weaknesses. For example, the S&T and industrial bases remain highly vulnerable to international economic fluctuations, as evidenced by the disruptions and regressions that have affected many of these countries since the 1970s because of the world recession and of changes in market conditions. In addition, the major economic role often played by the state in the economy, as a result of the development of bureaucracy, regulations and monopolies, discourages individual and institutional initiatives.

These difficulties are further complicated by the persistence of major social inequalities, so that further industrial growth depends on increased consumption by the wealthy or on increased exports. There is still a worrying lack of job creation in industry, owing to lack of productive investment or a tendency to favour highly capital-intensive investment in spite of the rapid growth of the labour force.

One additional feature is the failing or uneven development in the agricultural sector, with a majority of farmers still experiencing insufficient productivity gains.

As a result of these important characteristics, domestic demand stagnates, stifling the development of traditional industries or the emergence of new ones, and making it difficult to mobilize domestic financial and human resources.

One major feature of this group of countries must be kept in mind, because it directly affects future prospects: precisely because of past achievements, and because these countries are more integrated into international trade than others, most of them are highly sensitive and vulnerable to international trends. For example, greater future difficulties of access to foreign markets would require rapid promotion of domestic demand – in spite of the numerous social, economic and political obstacles outlined above. On the other hand, growing liberalization of international trade would demand an increasing degree of competitive specialization.

The following considerations provide the most relevant clues about the future course to be considered by these countries:

1. *High vulnerability of a growth strategy based on a domestic market confined to a minority, protection of some industry at the potential cost of lack of competitiveness, major export-oriented industrial projects controlled by multinationals, and rising unemployment as a result of the failure to create new jobs.*

2. *The development of long-term strategies based on a more egalitarian redistribution of the gains achieved (in terms of income and services, including education and training) in order to progress towards a social consensus and to lay the domestic foundations of development; stimulation and support of export-oriented activities by domestic entrepreneurs in agriculture, industry and services; skilful cultivation and management of the S&T base at all levels to promote diffusion of new technologies and exploitation, of opportunities for competitive specialization in promising areas.*

Overall perspective

Much of the above analysis underlines the importance of international relations in trade and co-operation in determining the future of the developing world. In addition, at the present juncture, the evolution of the indebtedness problem will undoubtedly directly affect the range of options open to a number of countries.

This being said, for most countries the course of future development will result from domestic choices – with the possible exception of the smaller land-locked countries deprived of natural resources and which are, much more than others, dependent on international support.

The crucial domestic choices to be made touch upon the very fabric of the societies concerned. A reorientation of national development strategies will set a high priority on the creation of a dynamic process of growth based on the production of goods and services, coupled with an expanding domestic demand and the removal of obstacles to private and institutional entrepreneurship. In other words, it depends on more egalitarian distribution of decision-making responsibilities, income and services. This of course raises the possibility of major socio-political upheavals affecting the balance of countries in the face of too-rapid development or stagnation, both of which exacerbate tensions.

The growing worldwide interdependence of national economies makes this threat a source of major concern to all, developing and developed countries alike. Discontinuities in the evolution of developing countries may have destabilizing impacts on distant industries. Conversely, industrialized countries have become more aware of the dangers of setting their own course without regard to the complex chain of events thus generated, with possibly catastrophic consequences for a number of countries throughout the world. These countries have had ample and bitter experience of the destabilizing impact on their own economies that they may suffer if they are not prepared to adjust to the competitive advantages gained by industrializing countries. It is thus in the interest of all to establish an international environment that will remove obstacles to development and facilitate the emergence of a consensus on solutions for the early prevention of potential conflicts and tensions related to trade – especially in the light of the need to design, as an integral element of development strategies, effective responses to major global environmental problems.

Thus, beyond the heterogeneity of situations and approaches, interdependence in the world economy entails a number of obligations for all the actors involved, ranging from industrialized to less-industrialized countries, and including transnational corporations and non-governmental organizations. What is at stake, at a time of renewed expectations that peaceful international relations will offer unprecedented opportunities for consensual approaches, is the design and implementation of new international rules governing competition and co-operation in order to create appropriate conditions for diverse development strategies and open the way to forms of aid better matched with the actual needs and requirements of recipient countries.

Science and technology obviously cannot solve all problems, but they play a decisive role in extending the range of options for consideration by countries and in providing building blocks for future development. The health and relevance of the S&T base also turn out to be especially important at this particular time, when the world is entering a new phase of economic growth largely prompted by technological advance. To benefit from the applications of S&T and ride the waves of productive change entails long-term multi-dimensional strategies focusing on all aspects of the innovation process, from basic general education to the training of scientists, engineers and managers, from the construction of a R&D capability as such, to the mobilization of research teams to tackle major national problems.

Bibliography

OECD. *Interfutures, Facing the Future.* Paris, OECD, 1979.
SALOMON, J.-J.; LEBEAU, A. *L'écrivain public et l'ordinateur,* Paris, Hachette, 1988.

SOEDJATMOKO. Towards a World Development Strategy Based on Growth, Sustainability and Solidarity: Policy Options for the 1990s. Paper presented at the twenty-fifth Anniversary Symposium of the OECD Development Centre, Paris, 6–8 February 1989.

UNESCO. *Statistical Yearbook 1988.* Paris, UNESCO, 1988.

UNITED NATIONS. *Demographic Directory 1985.* New York, United Nations, 1985.

WORLD BANK. *Development Report.* Washington, D.C., World Bank, 1988.

4. Policy challenges

The preceding discussion has shown that development policies can no longer be pursued regardless of the major scientific and technological advances which affect the economic, social and cultural future of countries around the world. It has also brought to light the fact that, as a result of national and international efforts, a number of countries and regions have built infrastructures to support scientific and technological research. And yet, on the whole, much remains to be done to incorporate science and technology as a lever for development.

This chapter will focus on this crucial problem of establishing a scientific and technological base that can make an effective contribution to development in general and, more specifically, to the solution of some of the most pressing problems currently confronting policy-makers in developing countries.

Towards an effective S&T base

Success in science and technology implies recognition of the specific requirements of scientific activity as an undertaking whose outcome is always uncertain, where failures must outnumber successes, which is painstaking and calls for ever more sophisticated equipment as well as continuity and concentration of efforts, and – last but not least – which depends on the creativity, morale, motivations and competence of scientists, engineers and technicians. Hence the importance of the provision of adequate human resources, selectivity in the choice of priorities, social recognition and support from the political system.

THE COMPLEX MANAGEMENT OF HUMAN S&T RESOURCES

The availability of skilled human resources is a crucial condition for the success of any development project. But the problem for each country is not merely to train these resources; it is to use them effectively and keep them in the country. The resources allocated to training will be of little impact if the people thus trained emigrate or do not use their skills to help the development of the country.

Two major difficulties confront Third World countries in this respect. First, the obvious attraction of the more advanced countries for the best trained people: better salaries, better living and working conditions, better prospects of professional growth, etc. Second, the lack of local opportunities to make full use of the creative capacities acquired, due either to the weakness and backwardness of productive structures, or to the deficiencies of the scientific and technical infrastructures. The result is not only an enormous waste of efforts, it is also a source of frustrations which feed emigration.

The very first steps to be taken to overcome some of these problems are usually outside the range of responsibilities of science and technology policy-makers. For example, the amount of investments in S&T, which in turn will determine the levels of salaries of researchers and technicians, is most often determined by budget offices; promoting the technological awareness of the very sectors which will allow or prevent the creative insertion of scientific and technical staff in productive activities falls under the purview of agricultural and industrial policies, etc.

In many cases, it will not be possible for a single country to tackle all these problems at once: a few may aspire to reach self-sufficiency in training; fewer still may eventually do so as far as centres of excellence in research and postgraduate teaching in certain key areas are concerned. In most cases – either because small countries will have to join forces with others, or because large and long-term programmes cannot be realistically pursued by a single country – the answers will have to be sought through co-operation.

This being said, training, at this time of rapid technological change, is a constant challenge throughout the world, in all countries, and a great deal of attention must be focused on the people who receive it, the subjects covered, the levels at which it is provided, etc. The emergence of new technologies requires radical changes in the philosophy behind training: this is indeed an opportunity that Third World countries cannot afford to miss, because their most vital interests are at stake. Diversity will be necessary to promote training demand and supply, with many different programmes of recurrent training, continued education, flexibility to shift from one discipline to another, variety in the duration and mix of studies offered (ranging from short vocational training to fourth-level education), availability of educational complements through extra-mural courses, mid-level technical training offering the choice between a first job or access to university courses, etc.

We recognize that many countries will hesitate to launch major programmes to promote training, because of the fear of a brain drain which seems to leave only two undesirable solutions: either to train at the best possible level scientists and technicians who will later on be attracted to the more developed countries, or to train them to a less advanced level so that their emigration prospects are lower. In fact, there can be no doubt about which path to follow. Only the first makes sense: 'second class' science and technology are not good enough. Excellence in the training of human resources must be an essential goal. But making the most of this resource is also of the highest priority, and requires specific strategies.

There is indeed a threefold challenge: training people properly, taking advantage of their training in productive ways, and maintaining their motivations to work in – and for – the nation. These conditions cannot be met without careful orientation of the science and technology effort. Wise choice of priorities thus plays a crucial role in the long-term health of the S&T base. The vision of the brain drain as 'Third-World pillage' is oversimplistic and out-of-date. It overlooks the fundamental responsibility of developing countries' governments to provide trained people with genuine career prospects and adequate working conditions, including a suitable institutional environment, legal status and sustained policy support.

It remains the case that the drain on valuable personnel can prove to be a disaster, especially for the smaller countries. When there is a past legacy of such losses, measures can nevertheless be taken to derive some advantage from the fact that nationals are working abroad in science and technology: contacts can be resumed and, if scientists and engineers cannot be brought back on a permanent basis, they can provide a source of information, advice and expertise for the domestic S&T effort.

For the future, to counter the threat of a brain drain obviously calls for strategies which extend beyond the mere provision of economic incentives (such as salaries or working infrastructures). Making scientists and engineers feel socially useful and directing their loyalties to the society as a whole, rather than adding to their material poverty a sense of the futility of the tasks carried out, should also be central elements of these strategies.

Although it is unthinkable to compete successfully in economic terms with conditions offered by developed countries to scientists, engineers and technicians, these people should find in their own countries minimum conditions of survival, both personal and academic. More precisely, this means that they should be able to devote themselves exclusively to scientific and technical activities, to pursue their research with reasonable assurance of continuous support for the duration of the project at the resource level originally agreed upon, in working conditions that are minimally appropriate as regards laboratory infrastructure, libraries, access to the relevant data bases abroad, etc., and with adequate provision and facilities for academic exchange within and outside the country.

Fourth-level studies should be an essential element in this strategy of scientific and technological development: they are the source of future generations of scientists and engineers. For this reason, they should be conducted in an advanced scientific research environment. This is only one of the essential dimensions of research in the higher education sector, which has other important functions, for example, as a channel for access to international scientific advances, or as a source of expertise for the assessment of the quality of the research work under way elsewhere, or yet again as an essential component in providing a suitable regional environment for development. Thus, the promotion of higher education should go hand in hand with the expansion of advanced research in the higher education sector.

This will prove difficult for the poorer countries. Sending students to highly developed countries is not necessarily the best solution. Regional co-operation in the development of postgraduate studies and research may often turn out to be the best – and in the long run the less costly – answer to this problem.

These policies will not fully succeed, however, unless active steps are taken to promote the social usefulness of the S&T personnel, and to foster actively the integration of the results of their work into production and essential services such as health, housing, transportation and education.

The brain-drain phenomenon and the frequent inadequacy of the responses offered by science and technology to the problems of underdeveloped countries may also result from the weak commitment of scientists and engineers to work on these problems, or from limited opportunities to do so. This reflects to some extent a lack of understanding of the issues at stake. Better awareness of the challenges to be met is in part a matter of socialization, but it also requires a greater involvement of the social sciences in S&T policies, which should seek to bring together representatives of 'hard sciences' and social scientists and promote a fruitful interdisciplinary dialogue.

This might also promote research workers' interest in the social and economic dimensions of technological change – an interest at present lacking in most developing countries, where 'social studies of science' often remain at best marginal. Conversely, however, it should be recognized that greater social awareness on the part of scientists, engineers and technicians will not suffice if they are not met half way by explicit social demands addressed to them.

THE MANAGEMENT OF SOCIAL DEMANDS FOR SCIENCE AND TECHNOLOGY

One of the most remarkable differences in the organization of S&T activities between Third World and industrialized countries relates to the institutional sources of funding and location of R&D efforts. The implications are serious, and affect the economic impacts of science and technology.

In general, financing of R&D activities by productive enterprises does not exceed 20 per cent of the total national R&D effort (in the case of Brazil), whereas such financing amounts to 50 per cent or more in many industrial countries, rising in Japan to three-quarters of the R&D effort.

There is a similar pattern as regards the percentage of scientists and engineers performing R&D tasks in the productive sector: in the relatively less-developed countries it is less than 20 per cent of the total S&T personnel; in the more advanced ones, it is over 50 per cent. Differences are even more marked with respect to scientists and engineers performing R&D tasks in manufacturing industry, as a share of the total scientific and engineering staff of the productive sector: in industrial countries they represent over 80 per cent; in the peripheral ones, they do not exceed 40 per cent – and only in exceptional cases.[1]

Several problems result from these structural characteristics, which usually tend to make the science and technology system a closed one:

The major R&D funding institution – the state – also employs a majority of the skilled staff. A very small part of the generally small number of engineers and scientists in the productive sector are employed by small and medium-sized firms, which constitute the bulk of the industrial sector. This makes the productive fabric of many countries structurally weak from the technological standpoint.

This weakness would not be so serious if there were a fluid transfer of knowledge from the S&T system to the productive system. This is precisely what seldom occurs, and the lack of information concerning productive methods, quality controls, new products, etc., co-exists with research that could make great contributions in those directions but does not reach the potential users. Engineers and scientists who would be in a position to identify problems and formulate demands on the S&T system are not sufficiently numerous in the field of production; moreover, there is an almost general lack of specialized structures to carry out systematic diffusion of knowledge and 'domestic technology transfers'.

1. NICs are an exception to this pattern: in Korea, for example, the percentage of engineers and scientists carrying out R&D tasks in manufacturing industry reaches 89 per cent.

Thus, in the absence of information channels, the S&T system is isolated from the socio-economic milieu.

It would be extremely dangerous, however, to conclude from the fact that a vast majority of R&D personnel are employed by the public sector that it suffers from hypertrophy which would justify a reduction. What appears to be hypertrophy merely reflects the co-existence of something weak with something that virtually does not exist. What is required is to ensure the emergence of productive sector R&D capacities without weakening the public effort but, on the contrary, strengthening it.

Thus a paradoxical situation emerges in many underdeveloped countries: their governments have a virtual public monopoly of financing and staff-hiring in the science and technology area – supposedly one of the key factors of productive performance – in the midst of market economies where production is in private hands. This is a result of the serious weakness of the domestic demand for science and technology.

The problems generated by this weakness of the S&T demand – at the productive as well as more generally at the social level – have not received sufficient attention. The demand for science and technology is usually taken for granted, without drawing a clear distinction between the implicit demand (what the productive system, and more generally the society as a whole, would require from S&T), and the explicit demand (what the various social and economic actors actually expect from S&T). In practice, there is a vast difference. How many people in developing countries realize that science and technology might provide answers to certain problems? How many people are capable of formulating specific concrete demands for S&T in relation to particular problems and expected solutions? There are many who cannot, and who can be found in key sectors of social and economic activity.

In this light, the challenge is twofold: to increase both supply of, and demand for, S&T. As in the case of training, policies implemented up to the present have essentially been concerned with supply. It should nevertheless be possible, in the framework of the balanced and comprehensive development policies which are suggested by this report, to stimulate the demand for scientific and technological activities and results.

Science and technology should thus not be seen as a luxury but as a necessity, and they should be treated as an investment, which requires a great deal of professional experience for the formulation and implementation of policies aiming at the development of endogenous S&T capabilities. This implies that resource allocations in this area should take account of long-term considerations, and that strategic decisions concerning national S&T efforts should rest with specialized government bodies.

THE MANAGEMENT OF PRIORITIES

The selection of priorities obviously plays an essential role in tuning the S&T effort to national needs, constraints and conditions. More specifically, as noted above, it provides a crucial dimension to training programmes and can also play a key role in fostering the demand for S&T and matching it with the endogenous supply. In the face of limited resources, this is by no means an easy task.

Almost all Third World countries need to increase the level of funding allocated to S&T, in many cases to multiply it by a factor of three or four to reach a minimum level of expenditure, of about 1 per cent of GDP. But many criteria of resource allocation should change as well. At present, in a typical situation, there are relatively substantial expenditures on equipment or infrastructure received through international co-operation, and a failure to provide adequate staff and decent salaries for the staff. Equipment is useless without people who have the motivation and the ability to use it.

The questions that this invites have been with us for decades: What are the subjects and sub-subjects to be tackled? Which technological developments should be fostered? What are the areas where fourth-level studies should be created? The answers – explicit or not – to these questions will determine the allocation of financial resources, and hence the creation of institutes, the implementation of projects, the training of human resources, etc., whose impacts will be felt for many years to come.

The structure of the decision-making process may be the source of many difficulties in the formulation and implementation of such policies.

There is in particular a lack of co-ordination between the different decision-making authorities and levels, leading to overlapping efforts, significant imbalances in the choice of research subjects, difficulties in the creation of interdisciplinary teams, etc. When they exist, co-ordinating bodies are often ineffective because their mode of operation is usually purely administrative in a narrow sense. One cannot 'co-ordinate' people without their consent. Bureaucratic decisions made 'from above' are not accepted by those who are immersed in the day-to-day requirements of scientific and technological work. As a result, a defensive strategy in the face of 'bureaucratic interference' has often even strengthened the relative autonomy of sectorial decision-making bodies and research institutions.

As a result, the pre-eminence of decisions stemming from individual interests limits the scope for institutional planning. It reinforces the lack of coherence between decisions made in the scientific and technological area and those which are made in other sectors of national activity, particularly those concerned with the development of the productive and service sectors.

It is thus not surprising that there are obvious deficiencies in the information base required for effective decision-making. Surveys on the scientific and technological reality are sporadic and non-systematic in most developing countries. When they are undertaken, these surveys are also, in general, of a routine nature which does not reflect the practical needs of decision-makers. For example, the number of holders of Doctor's and Master's degrees is more or less accurately established, but there is no attempt to gather information on research lines and their connection with subjects of vital national interest. In addition, surveys usually pay very little attention to qualitative aspects.

Prospective thinking and analyses of future trends and requirements are usually non-existent in spite of the need to set policies (for example with respect to education and training) in a long-term perspective. Such assessments would be needed, for example, to determine if biotechnology represents a promising area for a given country and – if so – what training programmes should be considered beforehand.

The selection or definition of priorities in the scientific and technological research field requires accurate and reliable information. In most countries, the quantitative and qualitative data base should be substantially improved, in terms of both updating and coverage.

There is a particular need for information on the current and future relationship between national and international realities. Prospective strategic studies in S&T can have a vital importance, yet they represent a peculiarly neglected field of policy-oriented research in the Third World. Such studies could be developed at national or international (regional) levels to:
Monitor international S&T trends.
Consider their economic and social repercussions.
Conduct comparative analyses of different science, technology and education policies.
Produce digests of the most important future-oriented studies carried out in different fields.
Discuss implications for the country or region concerned.
Produce periodic surveys of S&T innovations in the country and their main impacts on society.
Explore potential breakthroughs – in the creation of science and technology, in education and production – wherever they exist in the country. studying possible forms of back-up and assistance needed to facilitate their introduction and diffusion.
Highlight the most innovative and fruitful new ventures.
Promote periodical surveys of S&T capacity, with special attention to areas which future-oriented studies will have identified as of outstanding importance for the future.

THE CLAIM OF SCIENCE AND TECHNOLOGY ON POLITICAL WILL

A policy is as strong, legitimated and operational as the demand for its subject-matter is strong and structured. The weakness of S&T policies is thus intimately linked to the weak demand mentioned above. This is not unrelated to the lack of political will, which is reflected in the failure of broad institutional, social and economic support for S&T policies and of genuine consensus about their significance, their objectives, or their implementation.

There is a good deal of reference to 'political will' in discussions of development policies, but generally as a ritualistic statement, appearing at the end of a report in the form of: 'The things to be done, the measures to be taken, are clear. All that is lacking is political will.' It may be assumed that this inadequate political will is not easily generated, with a number of resulting problems, such as:

Failure to call upon national products and capabilities when they exist, rather than engaging in undiscriminating acquisition of foreign technologies without regard to possible implications for the future of the national S&T effort.[1]

Indifference of the major political and social actors to the implications of science and technology efforts, with a resulting lack of debate on these issues, non-involvement of the public in their discussion, and absence of social control over scientific and technological development.

Vulnerability of the scientific and technological enterprise to reactive decisions, fashion and 'stop-go' policies, which foster a sense of uncertainty – if not irrelevance – among researchers, and isolate them from the rest of the society.

Science and technology policies have a role to play in contributing to the emergence of 'political will' and a democratic debate on the future. For example, targets can be formulated in more explicit socio-economic terms to generate discussion; representatives of political, social and economic milieux can be called upon to participate directly in the formulation of these targets and the monitoring of programmes; and efforts can be made to increase general public awareness of the stakes involved in scientific and technological development.

1. These situations are fairly common in most developing countries, where the purchasing power of the public sector, instead of being used to promote endogenous scientific and technological development, is oriented towards the purchase of big and sophisticated 'turn-key' systems. This is doubly pernicious: on the one hand, it neglects unique training opportunities, and on the other, it introduces overcosts and inefficiencies, with little attention to basic problems such as implications for the environment, maintenance capacity, etc.

Harnessing science and technology to development

The implications of the worldwide diffusion of new technologies have been discussed above at some length, with particular emphasis on the need for developing countries to ride the new wave of economic growth. This is obviously easier said than done, when the old, perennial, problems are still with us and are often made even more severe by the profound changes affecting society and the economy.

Foremost among these changes, there is the process of 'dematerialization of production', which decreases the costs of materials and their transformation relative to those derived from intangible investments (research and development, training, data processing, etc.) thus drastically reducing the traditional comparative 'advantages' of underdevelopment: access to cheap raw materials and manpower.

This advantage becomes even less instrumental in the light of the central role increasingly played by innovation in the emerging pattern of economic growth, which increases the gap between the peripheral countries and the world sources of dynamism. The existing asymmetries between countries and regions are thus still reinforced.

And yet, in most cases,[1] there have been no specific policies in developing countries to cope with new technologies. Their introduction, in particular in the case of automatic data processing and communications, has been generally due to marketing by suppliers and not to a coherent, planned demand on the part of the countries concerned. When loans have been available – and they are acutely needed – they have usually been tied to the acquisition of specific equipment. This lack of policies coupled with insurmountable constraints has led to an accumulation of mutually incompatible equipment, to insufficiently trained specialists, to imports that 'lock in' entire countries with respect to future technological options and will prevent the emergence of endogenous capabilities, to a population with very disparate possibilities of access to the benefits of new technologies, etc.

To a significant extent, technology has been considered at policy levels because the mere possession of new technologies has acquired a mythical character with most political élites, who overlook the conditions required for their effective use: understanding their operation, the physical infrastructure and organizational conditions they require, the objectives they may serve and those they may not, the kind of training required for specialized personnel and the general public, etc.

Rapid full-scale exploitation of new technologies is thus unattainable.

1. There are, however, some examples of specific policies: Cuba, in biotechnologies, and Brazil and India, in micro-electronics and computer sciences.

90

Their mobilization to solve the specific problems of each country – which would offer a potentially enormous number of solutions – is greatly hindered, owing to the lack of research, of specialized training, of a capacity to generate and carry out projects, of knowledge accumulation to assist in the selection of technologies and in deciding where and how to acquire them. Methods which have been developed, in the framework of technology assessment efforts, to tackle these questions systematically are especially appropriate here, to assist policy-makers in the task of concentrating scarce resources in a way that will maximize benefits and minimize negative destabilizing impacts.

The relevance of technology assessment is reflected in its definition:

The whole body of activities and all the methods used to study as early as possible the different aspects and consequences of a technological or scientific development, preferably with regard to their interrelation, for various groups in the population, with a view to the social applicability of the technology or scientific discipline concerned.[1]

If this practice is viewed as important in central countries, it is obviously even more so in the Third World. Fostering the constitution of national or regional teams and developing technology assessment activities in close connection with future-oriented studies may be a highly efficient way to provide S&T policy with the qualitative information required for decision-making aiming at a better articulation of science, technology and development.

THE DEVELOPMENT OF ABSORPTIVE CAPACITIES

Policies to stimulate demand for science and technology are necessary, as noted above, in order to overcome structural weaknesses in this area. This entails progress in integrating technological considerations into the formulation and implementation of economic policies at all levels and in all sectors. The overriding goal is to raise overall absorptive capacities and awareness of possible benefits of science and technology, particularly in the industrial and public sectors as well as society at large. In each of these cases, policies will need to be adjusted to the specific natures of the groups and organizations concerned, which are so marked that it seems difficult, if not impossible, to design a common thrust.

1. Technology assessment activities may in fact extend to the social training of technical personnel. One of the tasks that NOTA, the Netherlands technology assessment group, considers of priority is the following: 'NOTA will also address itself to promoting the awareness of social responsibility among researchers in areas which involve the social and ethical aspects of scientific developments themselves, or which are concerned with the design, introduction and application of new or existing technologies.'

One of the main causes of weakness of demand and absorptive capacities in the industrial sector is a great lack of information, resulting from insufficient technical personnel in this sector. It will thus prove necessary to develop an active policy of information diffusion, involving the creation or strengthening of public technological laboratories whose services should include quality controls, different kinds of tests for products and processes, different advisory activities, with a particular stress on management and market aspects, etc. An active extension policy will also be required, involving visits to productive units by technical advisers who might suggest improvements in production methods, providing technical staff (conceivably under a 'shared-time' regime) and facilitating the incorporation of technology whenever it is deemed reasonable, etc.

Public sector attitudes towards S&T have long been recognized to be of central importance. In Third World countries, where private enterprises are generally of modest size, public administration is the only really powerful local client in the S&T area. Technologically complex projects, which offer opportunities for true learning processes and may have great social significance, can only be undertaken by the state. Policies in this area will stimulate more positive consideration of S&T if they call upon local participation in projects, forbid unjustified turn-key purchases, encourage planned growth of infrastructures while discouraging urgent last-minute acquisitions,[1] and ensure that public decisions are based on competent technical advice and that public programmes are adequately staffed with technical personnel. In view of their importance, these actions should be central concerns of science and technology policies.

The promotion of social awareness of the implications of technological advances is a basic factor in the health, vitality and relevance of the whole scientific and technological effort. In the face of technological changes which will deeply affect each citizen's everyday life and future prospects, the problem is usually to overcome an attitude of total passivity. The challenge here is mainly related to information and organization: to learn more about how to translate social concerns into technological demands and how to organize in order to respond to these demands. This will contribute to alleviating the most obvious inadequacies of changes which do not reflect people's needs, as well as enriching democratic practices. In pursuing these

1. In-depth studies should be carried out in key sectors of production or services, to assess potential impacts of the introduction of new methods and technologies. These assessments will thus contribute to the establishment of an informed national S&T demand in order to avoid unforeseen demands erupting in the midst of the greatest scientific and technical penury and calling for foreign technologies whose scope and sophistication are completely beyond the reach of local capabilities.

goals, science and technology policy can take advantage of existing networks such as schools, high-schools, townships and cultural centres.

This social dimension of S&T policies seems all the more important in the light of the increasingly acute problems faced by many developing countries as a result of the mushrooming of urban areas. Urbanization perhaps represents the greatest challenge in the effort to provide adequate services for a growing population, which often can be achieved only through the promotion of new technologies by public bodies. In this light, the management of urban areas represents one of the most – if not the most – difficult issue to be met by technology policies. It is also the greatest opportunity to make a new start: the design and diffusion of effective technological systems in this context will have enormous demonstration effects, and can prove to be a launching-pad for the growth of a new generation of industrialists, managers, scientists, engineers and technicians, fully aware of S&T opportunities and constraints. From this base, positive attitudes towards innovation can spread pervasively throughout the economy and society. For this reason, much of our discussion now focuses on technological policies in the urban context.

THE URBAN CONTEXT

In most developing countries, the social context, diverse and complex as it is, is characterized by rapid growth of social demands, linked with population expansion and the urbanization process; widespread poverty and growing urban unemployment in most countries; transfer of this poverty from rural zones to urban areas through migration (while these rural zones are largely left to fend for themselves); and increasing inequality in income distribution between social groups and between regions.

The rapid process of population concentration in urban areas is not only expressed by demographic changes concerning the geographic distribution of the population, or its concentration in cities of different sizes. It also entails changes in the modes of industrial and agricultural production, interrelations, patterns of distribution and consumption, social organization, the role of the state, the infrastructures and services required, and the role of technology as part of the problem or part of the solution.

While the degree of urbanization varies greatly at present in the different regions, the expected trend is to reduce these differences by the beginning of the next century, as shown in Tables A15 and A16 (see Appendix).

Population growth as such is not necessarily an alarming factor, what is alarming is the large number of people living in sub-standard conditions, as shown in Table A17. It can be roughly estimated that over 50 per cent of the urban population of the developing countries live in housing that does not provide adequate conditions for shelter, comfort and privacy. The population concerned do not as a rule have access to basic urban infrastructures and services such as piped water, sanitation, electricity, transport or communications.

THE TECHNOLOGICAL DIMENSION OF THE URBAN CRISIS

The most urgent task is therefore to give considered thought to the contribution that science and technology can make to the solution of the urban crisis. It is in the Third World cities – most often the capitals – that a large part of the problems referred to above are concentrated. At the same time, these cities usually contain the core of S&T activities, with most – if not all – of the countries' research teams and centres for creating, receiving, testing and disseminating new technologies.

Science and technology – in essence the technological innovation potential of the present decade – could be mobilized, at one and at the same time, in two ways to contribute to the alleviation of the problems outlined above: first, in seeking technological options that will absorb greater manpower without, however, sacrificing, as far as is possible, productivity levels and export capacity; and, second, in identifying new technological options for the provision of essential services such as housing, health care, food, power infrastructures, education, communications, urban management, transport and preservation of the environment, among others.

Studies dealing with the economic crisis of the present decade are innumerable. It may not be irrelevant to mention here those (e.g. Castells, 1985) that assert that the Western industrialized countries have overcome the crisis through a transfer of diseconomies to a large part of the developing world, which may thus be directly suffering from the social and economic costs of the technological and economic adaptation process implemented by the central countries.

Whatever the case may be, the fact is that, within a context of diminishing overall public expenditure, social-sector expenditure in most developing countries, particularly in Latin America and Africa, is falling rapidly. Retrenchment policies mean that urban social services budgets are reduced, curtailing in a radical fashion the quality and scope of supporting services, leaving the accommodation problem to be 'solved' by self-built solutions. Because of the drop in production and investment in the cities, unemployment and underemployment continue to grow. As a result, it can be said that most Third World cities are moving towards social fragmentation, the individualization of social processes and the polarization of urban territory and daily activities.

The situation is far from clear as regards the use of technologies in the city. It is obvious that technological 'fixes' alone cannot abolish social and economic imbalances in cities suffering from acute housing and services shortages as well as from environmental pollution. Technology as such will not suffice to ensure the competitiveness of an economy in the long term, or economic growth and full employment, or individual and community well-being. If technology is to contribute to these goals, it must form part of an overall process of social innovation (Martinez Pardo, 1988).

Thus, the social dimension of innovation cannot be ignored. It cannot be merely viewed as a linear technical trend, but should be considered as a social process, and technology as a social instrument (OECD, 1988). In this respect, there is no point in debating in the abstract the question of good or bad effects. What is at stake is the production model which generates innovations, diffuses them and puts them to use. The social dimension is all the more important given that application becomes more difficult in situations that differ radically from those for which a given technology was designed. This fact determines the social embedding of technology, and cannot be overlooked in the design of science and technology policies in developing countries.

Yet many surveys have shown that the use of technology in the cities of Third World countries responds to the supply of goods from producing and exporting countries, rather than to the needs of receiving countries. Technologies are thus incorporated in piecemeal and sectorial fashion, lacking any overall design.

Most town-dwellers usually have no opportunity to express their real requirements. In most cases, they are not even aware of the extent to which these requirements could be met by the application of modern technologies.

By contrast, the state has an important role to play. In most developing countries, public services are obviously unable to produce or distribute the full range of goods and services required by the growing urban population. In spite of the lack of appropriate administrative structures to cover all aspects of the services concerned, to anticipate future needs and make adjustments to original plans when necessary, public services still play a central role in providing a channel for a great number of economic and technological decisions. They should thus be viewed as key actors in the development of science and technology policies for the regions concerned.

It remains to determine to what extent technology policy could assist in countering the trends outlined above (incorporation of technologies unrelated to demand, mismatch between their supply and the real needs of the consumer public, piecemeal distribution by sector, absence of any control by society over technological decisions, exacerbation of the polarization of urban society, etc.), if it were harnessed to this goal by a decisive overall urban policy. There can be little doubt that, in the absence of such a policy, and even if the Third World succeeds in negotiating the present economic crisis, the existing divisions in society will become more acute. An élite may reap benefits from the new technologies, but the bulk of society will be excluded and will find itself unable to play its part in generating a virtuous cycle of growth and innovation. The risk is that the greater part of urban society will become passive consumers of these technologies or, worse still, mere outside spectators watching through a window the workings of marvellous machines which they do not understand, yet which have a profound effect on their way of life.

Four examples illustrate the difficulties, the urgent needs and the opportunities: housing, water supply and sanitation, transport and communications. In each of these cases it can be shown that a better response to the requirements of the lower-income groups is not only justified on social and ethical grounds, but can offer enormous opportunities for technology-based development.

HOUSING FOR LOW-INCOME GROUPS

A survey carried out in 1987/88 in Latin American cities showed that as far as the construction of housing was concerned, the accumulated shortfall plus new demands for accommodation meant that it was quite unrealistic to think that needs could be met from either public or private funding by using the technologies so far adopted. The resources assigned to traditional urban building and construction are not adequate, and public and private investment in 'official' building represent each year about half of what is really needed (Gutman, 1987).

The situation is far from being better in Africa: in Nairobi, around 40 per cent of the population lives in 'informal' housing; in Nouakchott, it is estimated that 45 per cent of city-dwellers live in precarious self-built housing. In Asia, the outlook is no less dramatic: 50 per cent of Delhi's population suffer bad housing conditions, as do 1.2 million people in Bangkok and 328,000 families in Manila (Hardoy et al., 1989).

Modern technologies are usually ignored in the construction of housing, particularly for low-income groups. Individuals who build their own houses with the help of families, friends and workmen engaged by them represent the main form of house-building in the low-income sectors.

The problem is not new. Twenty years ago (Hardoy et al., 1989), researchers in Latin American universities discussed which was the most convenient technology to lower construction prices and increase the offer of low-cost housing for the low-income populations. Most of the projects then developed remained on the drawing-board. The same situation affects to this day numerous research projects carried out in developing countries on alternative technologies in this sector. It may be assumed that construction firms are content with the current situation and do not feel the need, or find themselves in a position, to introduce technological innovations. Public standards often reinforce this situation, since they will only allow constructions built with traditional commercial materials.

WATER SUPPLY AND SANITATION

Water and sanitation are among the main problems of Third World cities, since they are closely linked to public health and the preservation of the environment. However, the population's needs are far from satisfied: in Freetown, Sierra Leone, only 50 per cent of the families have water taps, and only 5 per cent have flush toilets. In Nouackchott, more than two-thirds of the inhabitants do not have direct access to piped drinking water (Hardoy and Satterthwaite, 1987). In Latin America, the provision of drinking water and sanitation is at present one of the most inadequate services: in 1985, an estimated 25 per cent of the urban population (65 million inhabitants) had no piped drinking water; 40 per cent (105 million) were without any kind of sewerage (Faudry, 1988). Given the estimate that the urban population in Latin America will have increased by 50 million by the early 1990s, the figures for those without such services will still total 15 and 31 per cent respectively, even if the objectives of the International Drinking Water Supply and Sanitation Decade are met.

The present situation in Latin America with regard to water supply is that traditional systems – imported from central countries, such as the United Kingdom, Belgium and the United States – are generally too costly to become widespread. This is reinforced by the frequently large-scale, oversized nature of projects and their technical obsolescence, leaving aside any assessment of their practical suitability for everyday use.

Should we opt for less costly technical solutions? Researchers have identified a number of factors which circumscribe the range of options considered to only part of the existing technological range and which lead to adopting and installing the same systems as those long in use in Europe and in the United States. A basic factor is the type of training and information available to engineers, which locks them into the use of traditional techniques; another is the strategy adopted by powerful national and foreign firms in this sector. As regards transnational corporations, promotional emphasis on sophisticated technological equipment is sometimes backed up by offers of generous financial support. This is a fairly recent phenomenon, and it remains to be seen how far multilateral financing will ensure greater freedom of choice.

THE PROVISION OF TRANSPORTATION SERVICES

In most Third World cities, little attention is paid to public transportation. Sporadic changes in the transport systems, and the very great variety of technologies and vintages of technologies which may co-exist in the same town, reflect efforts to adapt on an ad hoc basis to the daily requirements of individuals in the struggle for existence. The end result is a form of social segregation, with inadequate services which are highly heterogeneous in nature and vary with the social class of the prospective users and the urban areas serviced. In many cases, transport systems are unreliable, and in general fall short of meeting the demands of users.

Latin America, which may be taken to be a representative case, has three major forms of public transport: city buses, suburban trains and subways. Buses are used by the majority of passengers including those in the lower-income bracket. Suburban train systems, used by the lower-income groups, are becoming run down due to inadequate financial and technological investment. Public subway systems, which are generally very expensive to construct and operate with larget deficits, are often underutilized, as in Santiago de Chile and Rio de Janeiro. It may well be that the subway is the only public transport system in the region which is not used principally by lower-income groups (with the possible exception of the Caracas subway).

It may be useful to recall here that studies have concluded that the development of subway systems often seems to have been determined by financial rather than technical considerations (Henry, 1985). Despite the occasional reference to technology transfer, rolling stock and equipment, the design and even the operation of systems tend to be exclusively foreign. On the other hand, the provision of the necessary infrastructure would mobilize the national construction sector.

THE DIFFUSION OF INFORMATION AND COMMUNICATIONS SYSTEMS

The most visible technological revolution in developing countries, which is spreading the most rapidly and possibly with the least social control, and which has important repercussions for all aspects of daily life, is probably that concerned with information and communications.

The theory that these technologies operate today as the motivating force and accelerator of the economic system has been a driving force behind the programmes carried out in the 1960s by the United Nations and UNESCO to speed up the development of communication networks in Third World countries (Lerner, 1985). It was based on the idea that exposure to the mass media would enable members of traditional societies to adopt the behaviour patterns of modern citizens, as had already happened in countries having attained an advanced degree of industrial development.

Despite programmes implemented to that end by UNESCO, the diffusion of communication technology has not yet had direct effects on social and economic structures, in creating a climate which could generate action to provide better living conditions for the population. The growth and modernization of the communication system coincided in many countries with a process of impoverishment of the great mass of town-dwellers, essentially due to the economic circumstances of the period. The change was mainly cultural. Nevertheless the technologies in question retain their full potential, multiplied by recent innovations, and may turn out to have a deep impact on the reformulation of solutions for developing societies, particularly in urban areas, with respect to the most deprived inhabitants.

Latin America offers a striking example of the present limits to the diffusion and application of these new technologies. Latin America was by far the best equipped region of the developing world in the first decade of computer expansion (58 per cent); Asia accounted for 28 per cent; the Middle East for 8.14 per cent; Africa for 5.37 per cent (Salomon, 1985). However, information technology has mostly been adopted in public administrations, and this type of computer use has not had a major impact on other sectors.

In Latin America, the fact that many public services adopted computers does not mean that they were computerized, or that the information concerning, for example, a city administration was available to civil servants or citizens. Yet there are some examples of effective systems developed on the basis of information technology, for example in Brazil. In São Paulo, the entire traffic-control system is now computerized; the same is true of the whole system of credit protection, and above all of the administration of income tax. On the other hand, it should be noted that services which have long been underfunded (education, health, social policy) are increasingly lagging behind, and that the budgetary and investment gap between these sectors and the more advanced ones tends to increase with the entry of Brazil into the information age.

The efficient operation of telephone networks is essential for the use of communication technologies, to provide access to interactive forms of communication, videotext, remote data processing, electronic mail and data banks, both nationally and internationally. The qualitative and quantitative differences between the developed countries and the Third World are very noticeable. In 1981, developed countries had an average of 46 telephones per 100 inhabitants, as against 0.8 in Africa, 2.0 in Asia (excluding Japan and Israel) and 5.5 in Latin America (Salomon, 1985). Most telephones are to be found in urban areas, mainly in capital cities.

As regards cable television, personal computers and especially videorecorders, the speed of change in developing countries follows consumption patterns that are different in each country, with the incorporation of technology taking place almost indiscriminately on the basis of the availability of supply from European countries, Japan and the United States. The social sectors with medium or high purchasing power are rapidly entering into the cycle of consumption of new communication technologies.

One of the most striking features of this evolution is the acceleration of certain social trends under the impact of the new communication technologies, in particular, for example, with respect to distance and segregation between groups with different levels of income and types of cultural capital. Technologies do not of course produce this polarization, but they give it added content and depth through uneven penetration and dissemination.

This may be the greatest obstacle to the successful articulation of new technological thrusts and development efforts: the technologies in question are 'network' technologies, whose attractiveness and influence increase exponentially with the number and variety of subscribers. Once again, the fact is that development strategies cannot succeed without broad redistribution of income, access to the benefits of technology and responsibilities.

Bibliography and references

AROCENA, R.; SUTZ, J. 1986. Unidad interdisciplinaria permanente de evaluacion prospectiva y promocion en ciencia, tecnologia y sociedad, fundamentos y propuesta de creacion. Study Document. FESUR, December.

ATAL, Y. 1989. Anticipating the Future: ASIA-PACIFIC Region. Paper submitted to the International Seminar: América Latina y el Mundo hacia el Año 2000, 30 April to 6 May. Quito, UNESCO.

CASTELLS, M. 1985. *High Technology, Space and Society,* Beverly Hills, Calif., Sage Publications.

FAUDRY, D. 1988. El agua potable y el sanemiento en las ciudades latinoamericanas, Un balance de la investigacion. In: *Medio ambiente y urbanizacion,* Vol. 7, No. 23.

GUTMAN, P. 1987. Urban Growth and Technological Change in Latin America: A Framework to Think the Future. *Cities* (London), Vol. 4, No. 2.

GUTMAN, P.; FINQUELIEVICH, S., et al. 1988. *Research Project: Urban Development and Technological Change in Latin America.* Part of the International Project 'Technological Prospective' for Latin America. Buenos Aires, CEUR-UNU-IDRC.

HARDOY, J., et al. 1989. *Conversaciones sobre la ciudad del Tercer Mundo,* Buenos Aires, Grupo Editor Latinamericano/ Instituto Internacional de Medio Ambiente y Desarrollo/IIED AL.

HARDOY, J.; SATTERTHWAITE, D. 1987. *Las ciudades del Terce Mundo: el medio ambiente de la pobreza,* Buenos Aires, Grupo Editor Latinoamericano/ Instituto Internacional de Medio Ambiente y Desarrollo/IIED AL.

HENRY, E. 1985. *Enfoques para el analisis del transporte urbano en América Latina. Transporte y servicios urbanos en América Latina.* Quito, CIUDAD-INRETS.

LERNER, D. 1958. *The Passing of Traditional Society, Modernizing the Middle East.* New York, Free Press.

MARTINEZ PARDO, M. 1988. Nuevas tecnologias, territorio y espacio local. International Seminar on Technological Change and Urban Growth in Latin America, Buenos Aires, 3–5 May. CEUR-IIED AL.

NOTA *Programme 1987.* Netherlands, NOTA.

OECD. 1988. *New Technologies in the 1990s: A Socio-Economic Strategy.* Paris, OECD.

SALOMON, J.-J. 1985. *New Technologies and Development,* Paris, UNESCO.

Conclusion

Three major developments have taken place around the world in recent years.

First, the governments of industrialized countries increasingly acknowledge the central role of science and technology in transforming the conditions of economic and social growth. They have become aware of the need to integrate S&T policies with all other fields of policy-making. Extending beyond the natural and engineering sciences, attention also turns to the social sciences, which are thought to have a crucial role to play at a time of rapid social change. Unfortunately, this acknowledgement is not yet universal, and seems to be especially lacking at policy-making levels in developing countries.

Second, the diffusion of technological advances throughout societies challenges traditional modes of administration. In science and technology, post Second World War policies had set broad priorities and left the running of scientific endeavours to the scientists themselves. The new importance of technology, and the multiplication of direct links between science, technology, the economy and society call for new approaches. The mere administration of science is no longer adequate. New management styles are required to maximize potential benefits. The administrative mode, which relies on hierarchies of priorities, objectives, processes and the like, is no longer compatible with the creative dimension of science. Science is viewed as a strategic resource in a market and process-oriented framework which operates effectively on the basis of decentralized responsibility, rapid adjustment, and far-ranging alliances with people and institutions outside one's own sphere of responsibility.

Third, the application of the new information and communication technologies is truly worldwide. New communications systems establish instantaneous modes of interaction for the industrial and business community from any part of the world to any other part, thus dramatically underlining the growing interdependence of national economies, to the

103

extent that the notion of national sovereignty is increasingly questioned as less and less relevant to the new realities. The telecommunications system has become the largest machine in the world and its impact on economic activities is potentially enormous. It will affect established structures, such as financial markets. It will generate many new activities previously unknown on this scale, in particular in services. A new world economy is being born, which holds many promises for those who will be able to participate – and the threat of exclusion from its benefits to all those who are not in a situation to become active operators and users of the new network.

In the face of these changes, the challenge of harnessing science and technology to development becomes all the more urgent, since the gaps between highly industrialized, industrializing and developing countries threaten to become even wider.

Science, technology and the development process

The challenge is not, however, simply to build up a sizeable science and technology base which could then be expected to contribute directly to development. Set in such terms, the agenda for action is deceptively simple. The reality is that the ability to draw upon the opportunities offered by the S&T base is determined by a whole array of socio-economic conditions which have to be met.

A dangerous type of dichotomy often prevails in many developing countries, where minorities benefit from industrialization while the majority are left in poverty, if not destitution. Decisive action is needed in this respect, not only on ethical and human grounds, but because the very possibility of endogenous development is at stake. This type of development is impossible unless domestic demand for goods and services increases and supports the growth of domestic industry.

Development will continue to be distorted, slowed down or prevented – and science and technology will not be able to contribute fully to endogenous and sustained development – until major social obstacles to the generation of a dynamic process of change are removed. This calls for decisive policies of structural reform and response to the requirements of the poor sectors of the population, ranging from jobs and basic services to democratic participation in local and national decision-making, and including the safeguard of the basic civil liberties.

Thus, there is a 'hidden agenda' beneath the purely technological issues. It touches, on the one hand, on the much less tangible cultural and institutional preconditions and arrangements which accompany or precede effective economic and technological development. It also deals in particular with the role assigned to science and science policy in developing countries within the process of absorption and development of technology, as a further 'intangible' pre-condition for catching up.

A society's general attitude towards scientific approaches and the possibility of taking advantage of them is inextricably linked to its basic cultural patterns, which affect its overall positive or negative sensitivity to scientific thinking and its ability to consider change as one of its options.

We believe that there is no universal cultural model which would be a necessary condition for the exploitation of the opportunities offered by science and technology. Each culture can – and should – retain its integrity. However, in the modern world, each culture is increasingly confronted with the challenge of science and technology, and must find its own way of responding to it. Numerous examples show how dangerous, and ultimately self-defeating, it may be to attempt to inject science and technology forcibly into an unprepared culture. Steps must be taken to progress towards a better collective awareness of science, and avoid traumatic alienation and rejection.

We suggest that popularization should be one of the very early steps of a national S&T policy, directed to all groups of society and based on the development of scientific and technological themes in the media, including the diffusion of special periodicals.

Supplementary measures would include the development of public libraries and the creation of S&T museums. Open days could also be organized with national scientific institutions. Public discussions of the social and economic implications of the S&T effort could be developed, with the participation of scientists, engineers and technicians.

Institutional pre-conditions for catching up range from the obvious ones, such as levels and spread of education or the diffusion of technical skills in a society, to very complex ones, which are intricately bound up with historical development, its continuities, and especially its discontinuities, within a society.

If, for example, the West began its rise from an economic and technological position somewhat behind that of Chinese and Islamic civilizations of the same period, the many factors contributing to the Western success story include such institutional arrangements as the early separation of the political and economic spheres or economic decentralization. Two patterns of economic growth have been instrumental as a result: one associated with an expansion of trade and economic resources, and the other primarily attributable to scientific and technological innovation, beginning essentially in the eighteenth century.

As the history of science and technology in the West shows, scientific activity was not originally undertaken in response to economic needs. For most of Western history, science and industry might have existed in different worlds. However, science and technology became the key factors shaping and fuelling economic growth as a result of the gradual linkage of innovative activities in such different spheres as public service and utilities, economic enterprises and science. This linkage was achieved through institutional arrangements and mechanisms such as decentralization of authority and scientific autonomy as well as the emergence of professionalization as a set of rules, attitudes and behaviour – a development which ushered in a new period, with innovation becoming a major determinant of economic growth.

Innovation was in fact increasingly defined in a wide sense, to include experimentation (inventions and their further systematic development) within science, as well as 'experimentation' within the economic sphere, with respect to new products, methods of manufacturing, types of enterprise, organization of market relations, the transport and communications systems, etc. In other words, a blend of technological and social innovations highlight the extent to which institutional configurations played a decisive role in 'how the West grew rich'.

Thus, institutional configurations cannot be taken for granted as being unrelated to technological evolution. It is no accident that it is precisely when new technologies are spreading throughout the world economy that industrialized countries devote so much attention to the need to integrate science and technology policy concerns into all sectors of government action. The institutional framework of the embedding of science and technology may of course be of decisive importance for the inception of innovations and the capacity to absorb them into the economic and social spheres by translating them into products, processes, forms of organization, etc. But it becomes even more decisive for the subsequent diffusion phase, which entails a host of consecutive incremental innovations and adaptation processes, without which no particular innovation (not to mention large, pervasive socio-technological systems) could spread into the economic and social strata.

The dominant views of the role of science and technology in development do not account for this complexity of interactions. One side argues for a pragmatic short-term, economic-benefit-oriented approach with emphasis on international technological (import) linkages. Another argues for a more universal orientation and emphasis on indigenous scientific development, which may be an important strategy to enable developing countries to participate in what is, after all, a shared cultural heritage of humankind. These divergent viewpoints reflect a dilemma that scientists in developing countries know only too well, a dilemma between a 'local' orientation, geared to practical, useful and relevant work, yet which carries little prestige and rewards from the international scientific community, or that of maintaining an international orientation and identity but becoming at the same time alienated from the national context.

This dilemma is acutely felt on an individual as well as on a collective level. It can be traced to the fact that science in developing countries (again with a few exceptions) is often felt to be capable of no more than a very limited contribution to the total knowledge flows that transform local cultural, social and economic conditions. Science, as an instrument for change whose potential import rests primarily with the scientists themselves, is thus not connected with the user environment as it is in the industrialized countries. Independent of the pressing, immediate needs in different national contexts, a fundamental question has to be faced: how, in the long run, a social and economic context can be generated which allows science to take root in developing countries and appropriate pre-conditions be generated for the effective absorption, adaptation or indigenous development of technologies, production methods, etc.

It is clear to us that such a long-term comprehensive strategy rests on an explicit national commitment to reinforce local scientific as well as technological efforts: the former because it is the 'seed corn' which will generate new innovative capabilities; the latter because it provides the key instrumentalities needed to attack local problems; and both because their multiple interactions are decisive for the absorption of new ideas and methods as well as for the training of new generations of scientists and engineers.

The S&T potential as a whole is a strategic resource which must be carefully created, exploited and managed to be able to make its contributions. But this does not mean that excellence in science can only be pursued without reference to local problems and conditions. It is the task of the managers of the S&T base to avoid the pitfalls of trivialization of research on the one hand and irrelevance on the other.

A first condition is a clear understanding of what science can and cannot achieve. There is no one-way causality link between scientific capability or level of commitment and investments in science, and economic growth and development. It may well be that the quest for 'scientific' solutions to some of the developing countries' acute problems will often turn out to be pointless: there are many areas where science does not – and cannot – offer simple answers.

The promotion of scientific approaches, in financial as well as in institutional terms, is another important condition for full participation in a universally shared heritage which holds the keys to further relief of poverty and betterment of human conditions, as well as to the sustainable global development of natural resources. This heritage is not only the body of accumulated human knowledge, but a set of methods and mechanisms to arrive at new concepts and conclusions.

The role of science and technology has to be seen as crucial in a larger cultural, social and institutional context, which determines the potential for implanting indigenous social choices rather than responding to (i.e. importing) the technological choices stemming from market and social clearing processes in the developed world. International competitive pressures on individual countries can be enormous, forcing them to base their development strategies on the international availability of certain technologies, or on the limited opportunities offered by the exploitation of specific commodities and endowments, rather than striving for more balanced, overall development. Endogenous science and technology capabilities, in this respect, will offer increasing 'margins of liberty' for choices more closely tuned to national requirements and the attempt to diversify the economic base.

These considerations are all the more relevant at the present time, when the rapid progress of technologies, industries and services may present developing countries with new windows of opportunity: on the one hand, the opportunity to apply emerging new technological solutions to perennial problems (as in the case of biotechnologies in relation to health) and, on the other hand, to participate in the generation and the improvement of technologies. The latter presupposes, however, a sufficient command of scientific and technical knowledge.

It may well be that those countries that have at least partially achieved such a command, and are not hampered by the structural weight of 'old industries', may be better able to define and implement new technological trajectories which will not be stifled by co-existence with older technological regimes in terms of actual production, investments, skills and organizational and institutional embeddings. There may be many cases where the costs of entry at the start of a new technological development will turn out to be fairly low as regards experience or managerial capacity and capital requirements (in contrast to the import of capital-intensive mature technologies).

However, two additional requirements would have to be met: first, to overcome or to compensate for the lack of locational and infrastructural advantages; and second, to dispose of the scientific and technical knowledge required to make use of these opportunities. While much of the knowledge required to enter a new technology system in its early phase is public knowledge (available at universities, for example), it is also apparent that many of the skills and incremental improvements necessary for the successful introduction and subsequent diffusion of a new technological system can be acquired only by a process of 'learning by doing'. In such circumstances, science policy in developing countries should not only be concerned with the appropriation of (in principle free) public knowledge at the international level, but also of how this knowledge can effectively be translated to respond particularly to national and local requirements for new processes, products and services.

Technological innovation processes could thus offer an opportunity to break out, especially (possibly only) in the very early phase of the life cycle of a newly emerging technological system, i.e. in the transition period to a new development phase in which the ultimate characteristics and trajectories of economic growth and catch-up opportunities are being formed. However, this puts an even greater premium on being prepared to perceive and seize the opportunities which thus arise : any developing country that can take advantage of this sort of opportunity must have developed a position (probably through decades of efforts to acquire mature technologies) to dispose of sufficient scientific and technological capabilities and skills, as well as supportive institutional frameworks.

From the viewpoint of this report, the agenda for action of developing countries with respect to science and technology is thus threefold: to create a scientific and technological base; to use it in an appropriate way; and to manage it. A final section will discuss the role of international co-operation in this context.

A preliminary statement of caution should, however, be made at this point. One of the essential themes of our report is to underline the fact that each country should recognize the uniqueness of its situation and formulate its own development strategy. There are no ready-made recipes or models. Countries have been brought together in certain groups because they seemed to share common features. But we are fully aware that there are also often significant differences and variations between countries. Thus, in particular cases, suggestions addressed to a group of countries may also be quite appropriate to the special situation of a country included in another group. In this spirit, priorities are often suggested under the assumption that resources will be so limited that they will compel policy-makers to focus only on the most urgent tasks. It may well be that, for example, in Group A countries international aid or other sources will enable some countries to develop a more diverse range of targets.

The creation of the S&T base

A large number of developing countries, which this report has attempted to identify (Group A – see Chapter 3), have yet to take the first steps towards the promotion of a science and technology base. These countries are generally characterized by all or most of the following features: very low income per inhabitant, a share of less than 0.3 per cent of GNP devoted to R&D, less than 100 R&D scientists and engineers per million population, less than 20,000 potential scientists and engineers altogether, and less than 200 third-level students per 100,000 inhabitants. In many cases, information on science, technology and education is lacking or not coherent. This lack is, in itself, proof enough of the scant attention paid to the matters in question and to the fact that they do not appear, in an informed manner, at the top of the political agendas.

The collection of relevant, accurate, detailed and recent indicators of scientific, technological and educational activities is a necessary condition for effective development policies based on accurate assessments of the strengths and weaknesses to be taken into account. High priority should be assigned, at national and international level, to the production, on a continuing basis, of an adequate data base in the areas concerned.

We suggest that, in view of the limited resources available, the creation of a research base cannot be realistically pursued as a primary goal for these countries at their present stage of development. Research teams which have been established find themselves isolated in an uncongenial environment and powerless to attack effectively the problems at hand, develop solutions, and have them considered by the relevant groups. Furthermore, societies that are not in a position to take advantage of the available scientific and technological resources are not likely to provide research with the kind of long-term consistent support which would be required. The creation of basic conditions necessary for applying science and technology and the process of building up a research and development base are, in principle, two aspects of the same process and should be pursued in conjunction when possible.

Foremost among these basic conditions, we stress the need to build up general education. In particular, it should be clearly understood that it is not enough to make special provision for the training of young scientists and engineers, although this is obviously an essential need for the future.

The notion of an adequate educational base for future scientific and technological efforts extends far beyond this, to the training of future personnel and leaders in government, industry, services and agriculture, who

110

will be able to assess and seize, from their respective professional perspectives, the opportunities offered by science and technology. What is essentially at stake here, therefore, is not the production of a scientific and technological élite, but the enormous task of increasing the general public awareness of the major implications of development.

We strongly suggest that the primary asset for future development and growth, in any country, is the level of education and training of its general population and of its professionals and workers, in all spheres of activity.

Efforts to raise this level to the maximum should be of the highest priority for national governments, as well as for international co-operative undertakings.

It therefore follows that the creation of R&D capabilities should not necessarily be considered to be a top priority for developing countries which have not yet achieved the basic conditions required to promote these capabilities and take advantage of them. The creation of such a research potential should be pursued as a complement to the basic conditions outlined below.

Such an overall policy focus does not necessarily imply, however, that the future cannot be prepared and the first steps taken towards developing endogenous scientific capabilities. Important investments for the future might, for example, consist in the first elements of a scientific and technological infrastructure. But these steps should be carefully devised in order not to strain existing resources but to open the way, on a modest scale, for developments to come.

Special attention should be paid, in particular, to the design of third-level educational institutions so that they have a potential for growth and diversification. Technical and engineering schools should be provided with state-of-the-art machinery and equipment, and particular attention should be paid, in curricula, to the maintenance of this equipment. Other investments which will subsequently prove invaluable for domestic science and technology include, for example, the creation at an early stage of scientific and technical libraries which can begin to acquire the material needed not only for education in science, but also for future research.

Promising science students should be offered the opportunity to pursue their studies abroad in order to acquaint themselves with research, under schemes that include incentives to return home after their training.

The scope of scientific activities is broader than R&D as such. It includes, for example, technical support such as quality control, testing, advice and maintenance of advanced equipment. In many cases, it will be most useful to establish such capabilities to assist agricultural populations in fighting local pests and diseases and to make better use of local resources and materials.

Technical support centres should be established, nationally and internationally, in close liaison with third-level educational institutions as well as professional and vocational training schools. They should be adequately equipped, and staffed with competent technicians. They should clearly not be research bodies, but should be able to tap the international pool of knowledge for solutions which they should test before implementing them at large. Students should be encouraged to participate in these activities, which would make them more aware of the problems of the community and the potential of S&T to assist in solving these problems.

Some of the countries that still lack the first foundations of an S&T base are nevertheless commodity exporters or have a relatively important manufacturing sector, as pointed out in Chapter 3. Special consideration should be given, in such cases, to the potential contribution of S&T to greater effectiveness and diversification of ongoing economic activities.

Careful analysis of the potential for future growth is, in itself, a research effort which should be encouraged to identify potential threats and opportunities. It is especially important that the necessary expertise in economic analysis be acquired and strengthened as a source of advice for the formulation of future strategies.

Technical support centres, along the lines discussed above, could be established by governments to respond to the technological needs of small manufacturing industries, identify their economic problems, conduct studies and surveys to bring to light new challenges, and recommend suitable policy adjustments.

This would also include advice on the acquisition of foreign technology and on the negotiation of licences, as well as technical assistance for the utilization and maintenance of equipment.

Special mention should be made here of the case of very small countries – the 'micro-economies', whose populations range between 100,000 and 1.3 million. It is generally taken for granted that the exploitation of scientific and technological opportunities calls for abundant resources. In other words that 'big is effective'. Although it is undeniably true that only the larger and wealthier countries can afford to explore the broad range of issues at the frontiers of science and technology, it remains the case that highly selective strategies, based on narrowly-defined goals directly related

112

to local conditions, can also be highly rewarding. The example of Iceland – with a population of 220,000, one of the highest living standards in the world and one of the most advanced agricultural and fisheries technologies – deserves to be quoted here as a confirmation that, even for the very small, the highest ambitions are not out of reach. One can only point out, however, that this success is built on solid foundations which include a very high level of education, a great deal of entrepreneurial spirit, careful strategic allocation of resources to technology-related efforts and active involvement in many international co-operation schemes.

The achievement of a high level of education throughout the population, the establishment of adequate technical infrastructures to support local economic activities, the ability to integrate strategic planning and policy-making at the highest level, and the systematic co-ordination of local with international efforts are vital pre-conditions for development in the smaller countries.

The exploitation of the S&T base

A number of countries have already acquired the basic elements of an S&T base (Group B – see Chapter 3). These countries devote more than 0.4 per cent of their GNP to R&D, they have between 100 and 250 R&D scientists and engineers per million population and between 20,000 and 80,000 potential scientists and engineers. They also have between 200 and 900 third-level students per 100,000 inhabitants.

In this light, these countries can be said to have an emerging scientific community, although in many cases its members – not to mention government agencies and other institutions which employ scientists – are not necessarily themselves aware of it. Yet, a self-aware and well-organized national scientific community will prove to be a great step forward in providing opportunities for mutual contacts and exchanges perhaps leading to common projects; in facilitating contacts with colleagues abroad; and in exploring new ideas, jointly with potential clients, in order to recommend new projects which could usefully be launched to exploit the results of previous or ongoing work.

Although, in the development of such communities, much depends on the initiatives taken by the scientists themselves, various steps can be taken by public authorities to make more explicit the importance attached nationally in S&T work, and thus open the way for such initiatives.

The resources allocated yearly to R&D by the different public agencies should be brought together each year in a single document, as a 'science budget', and presented for discussion by Parliament with a government statement on its implications for the national S&T effort and overall development thrust.

We stress the importance of this 'science budget', which should not be a purely formal exercise. As such, it will provide a general perspective on the public R&D effort and will make it easier to debate priorities. It will demonstrate the interest that government places in S&T as important instruments of national development. It will provide an important source of information on the national S&T effort, will bring to light possible gaps in public efforts, and may prompt private initiatives to complement them.

The preparation of the 'science budget' is thus, in our view, an essential element of the national S&T strategy. Its message would be clear: drawing up such a clear statement of the strengths and weaknesses of the public effort would in itself present evidence, domestically as well as internationally, of the seriousness and realism with which policy-makers view the S&T effort as a long-term investment and of their determination to take full account of its needs and opportunities.

The 'science budget' may thus be a necessary first step towards the establishment of a national consensus on an S&T-based national design or vision of the future. It is essential to recognize from the outset that such an outcome can only be brought about by the joint efforts of research workers and policy-makers, and special efforts should be made to bring them into close co-operation.

In the preparation of the 'science budget', scientists and engineers should be invited to comment and present recommendations. If there are no suitable bodies representing the whole community of research scientists and engineers, a special commission could be created on as broad as possible a representative base to organize this consultation. Public agencies responsible for some parts of the R&D effort should also have to produce annual reports on these activities, as important inputs to budget discussions.

Unfortunately, many of the scientists in question are still primarily preoccupied by the need to struggle in order to live on their income, obtain the minimum means required to do some research, and communicate with colleagues abroad. Under such conditions, there can be no community of scholars in the true sense of the word. In addition, needless to say, there can be no real community (but at best several communities) when the nation itself is not united by a common faith in its future and a sense of common purpose.

The professionalization of researchers must be founded on adequate means of livelihood, career prospects and effective working conditions, which include continuous flows of communication with colleagues at home and abroad. We suggest that the maintenance of minimum satisfactory standards in all these respects should be a prime concern of government policy in science and technology.

It remains the case, however, that whatever the level of awareness of scientists as a community in a given society, the harnessing of S&T to the solution of urgent development problems will not be achieved by the single-minded pursuit of research subjects selected in the light of worldwide developments in the disciplines, but by the promotion of endogenous scientific and technological responses to particular ecosystems and to specific socio-economic situations. The process of selection of adequate responses hinges on choices made at all levels, from the development of national political priorities to the daily tasks of running research projects. It cannot be solved by authoritarian decisions, but by a process of awareness-building.

It is expected, for example, that by the end of the century most of the Third World population will be located in large urban areas. There are enormous implications for policies which attempt to cope with unemployment, food production and delivery, education, sanitation and health, waste management and environmental control. The development of the basic infrastructures needed should reflect the need to develop and implement sustainable development strategies that are in harmony with the environment, conserve the physical resources base and involve new approaches to education and services.

A basic observation needs to be made at this point: the notion of science as a basic resource for development refers to the whole system of disciplines, ranging from the natural and life sciences to engineering sciences, and including the social sciences. In most cases, the problems to be solved by developing countries will call for the joint contributions of several disciplines. It will often turn out that social scientists, in particular, will make important contributions through their involvement in policy studies, area studies, cultural studies, etc. , whose results may directly affect crucial technological decisions and thus prevent the repetition of some of the major mistakes of the past. Their inputs will be fundamental for the design of institutions in particular programmes, and more generally for the definition of balanced development strategies.

More fundamentally still, social scientists can bring to light the structural features of society which directly affect the emergence of new problems and the collective ability to solve them. They thus contribute to increasing awareness among the general public of new challenges and help set the stage for balanced development.

The social sciences have a key role to play in the formulation and implementation of policies to tackle the enormous problems which are emerging. The promotion of social research in developing countries should be accompanied by efforts to involve natural scientists, life scientists, engineers and social scientists in joint attacks on the problems in question.

The need to steer S&T policy towards local opportunities, problems and constraints obviously does not mean that Western contemporary science as a whole is irrelevant in so far as the challenge of development is concerned. Far from it. It does mean, however, that the thrust of efforts in industrialized countries may not reflect all the priorities suggested by the economic and social conditions of developing countries.

A balance must be struck between local requirements and the need to be well informed about the major movements in international R&D. Academics and teachers will play a vital role in this process, provided that they are not cut off from other actors in the national scientific and technological efforts, and that their awareness of international trends will be shared on a continuous basis with other interested groups in the population. In addition, the group of scientists concerned should not, in the process, be diverted away from its basic responsibilities in education. This underlines once again the importance of investing in a broad educational base. But more diversified efforts are needed to achieve a satisfactory balance of the skills which are now required.

One approach which could be extremely fruitful would be actively to seek to increase the number of international scientific meetings hosted by developing countries. This would provide more opportunities for the members of the local community of teachers, scientists and engineers to establish contacts with foreign colleagues. Such events, if they were well publicized, could also raise awareness of scientific and technological issues among the general public. International exhibitions might also be very beneficial in this respect. Obviously, international assistance will often be required.

Better understanding and monitoring of world developments in science and technology, however, cannot be left entirely to chance. Diplomatic missions abroad should be expected to provide information of major scientific and technological developments on a routine basis. Special inquiries should be undertaken regularly by groups representing the main national or regional interests involved, to acquire first-hand knowledge of the most important trends.

These mechanisms will be effective only in so far as the information gathered is rapidly made available to all concerned. The constitution of effective networks of communication and collaboration between researchers and potential users of research results has become, in all countries, a key factor in establishing a pattern of rapid response of research to needs, and of the production sector to new opportunities.

The creation of such networks is a necessary condition for the successful exploitation of new knowledge and know-how. In many cases, networking can only be achieved by overcoming long-standing social and intellectual prejudices. Governments have a key role to play in providing opportunities for bridge-building between groups that ignore each other.

Training programmes, at national and international levels, can foster the development of such networks and promote the special skills and experience needed to assess new opportunities and constraints in the light of specific requirements, resources and capabilities. These training programmes should be addressed to scientists and engineers involved in R&D activities, as well as to government officials and industrialists.

Overall, the responsiveness of the social system to new opportunities generated by scientific and technological progress should be encouraged. In many cases, the successful exploitation of new knowledge can be traced back to the initiative of individual(s) who have acted out of self-interest. The existence of incentives which will encourage individual initiative is essential.

Traditions and regulations often discourage individuals interested in exploiting a new idea or launching a new undertaking. Regulations which affect the behaviour of employees in government services, in universities and in industry should be adapted to increase rewards for creative initiatives, and to allow for cross-fertilization between different sectors, for example to make it possible for teachers to participate in other activities.

Such an approach calls for a spirit of institutional experimentation, diversification and investment in order to achieve the institutional base that will foster growth in local S&T systems. The nature of the objectives to be defined when building such an infrastructure for research will obviously vary with local constraints and opportunities, but should also take account of the international context and provide for bridges to be thrown across the international scientific and technological efforts.

Institutions that undertake long-term strategic research (on urban problems, energy, etc.) are especially important to bring convergent efforts to bear on spe-

117

cial national problems. Such institutions should be reinforced when they exist, and created when needed. They should be maintained at the highest level of quality in order to establish productive linkages with relevant research groups abroad.

What is at stake is the achievement of a state of adequate preparedness, with the ability to define priorities, implement and achieve them, import technology when needed and, after careful consideration of all alternatives, use traditional resources wisely, relying on the best science to build upon available resources.

One important challenge for all countries is to make provision for adequate investments in institution-building to address different regional needs at subnational level. In this respect, the concept of critical mass is of crucial importance. The presence in a given institute of a handful of scientists covering a broad range of disciplines may have a symbolic value, but it does not meet the efficiency requirements of research efforts. It is better to concentrate a team of an adequate size (which may vary according to disciplines and areas) on a relatively limited range of problems and themes reflecting medium- and long-term national priorities. It is equally important that provision be made for the technical infrastructure, including technicians as well as equipment, and for continued adequate funding for the day-to-day activities of the group. Science can be an expensive activity and initial investments will bear fruit only if the requisite means are provided on a regular basis.

The effective use of science and technology as a resource base will call for concentration of R&D resources in a few strategic areas, in order to achieve critical mass effects, and open the way to substantial interaction between researchers, and between researchers and clients of research. These clients – domestic industry, subsidiaries of foreign firms, as well as government departments – should be encouraged to open contractual relationships with research teams.

The management of S&T resources

A third group of countries (Group C – see Chapter 3) has already acquired a relatively significant S&T base, which can be mobilized for development provided it is managed with due regard to the peculiar requirements of research and to the complexities of the innovation process. This group includes a number of countries with sizeable commodities exports and an expanding manufacturing sector which constitute an economic and technical potential for the absorption of new technologies. Many of these countries, however, have suffered economically in recent years, and many past accomplishments have been somewhat dislocated: although they still have a significant force of S&T personnel, the growth of educational and research institutions has slowed down and has often even become negative. The danger is, of course, that more and more scientists will move abroad, and that it will become increasingly difficult to regain the ground that has been lost.

No country can afford to let its scientific institutions decay. Reconstruction of what has been allowed to deteriorate in this area is of the highest priority. National and international efforts should focus on generating, throughout the education and research systems, a new sense of dynamic growth and momentum.

The injection of additional resources is indispensable. Science, however, does not produce economic and social benefits automatically. Results do not happen miraculously but as a result of careful management of the resource. Like a suitable fertilizer in agricultural soil, it may be a necessary condition, but it does not produce crops by itself. Other inputs are required to achieve the best combination of factors in which science and technology may have larger or smaller parts to play, according to local conditions, traditions and opportunities. There is no single chain of identical actions. There are many different roads to be travelled in order to reap the benefits from scientific activities. The basic heterogeneity of development trajectories is open to a great deal of variation and creativity provided the basic requirements are acknowledged. The multiplicity of approaches, in a worldwide perspective, is in fact a source of creativity and increases the chances of success. Resources are scarce, and a single nation cannot keep all options open. Heterogeneity will make it possible to learn from the successes and failures of others.

There are no ready-made models or recipes. If there is one lesson to be learned from the broad range of different development success stories to date, it is that accomplishments are built upon a foundation of high-quality training and general education coupled with the will to exploit comparative advantages and strengths. Each country must clarify its own original choices in this respect at an early stage, join with others, if need be, to achieve greater effectiveness, and maintain at all costs the will to implement its design over the long term.

The definition of priorities should evolve during the development process. It should reflect the fact that not all developing countries will be able to become industrialized and exporters of manufactured goods from the outset. 'Late-comers' should be encouraged and obtain support in order to be in a position to develop in accordance with their 'vocation' – taking account of area, population, natural resources endowment, geographic location, historical and cultural roots, etc.

At this point, it seems necessary for us to underline the problem-solving or transforming character of the new development strategy suggested here. In view of the fact that another version of Keynesian development strategies on a worldwide scale seems hardly probable, and that the continuation of 'status quo' policies may lead to disaster for all, the conception and implementation of new strategies will be of paramount importance for the survival of the global system. These new strategies should be based on the premise of diverse and evolving national approaches to the development challenge.

This being said, one of the most difficult problems for each country and region is to select wisely the areas to be explored by endogenous research and the technologies to be imported. This involves very fine tuning in the design of priorities and in their implementation, in order to draw as much as can be drawn from the accumulated world experience and knowledge base, while leaving as much scope as is feasible to the development of national competence and expertise.

On many occasions, selective decisions will have to be made, since extremely advanced technologies may be required in certain cases (for example, satellites for education purposes), while less sophisticated approaches may be sufficient for other purposes.

The acquisition of a given technology abroad is often not the result of lack of competence at home in the area in question, but of the feeling, which may or may not be justified, that domestic products are of inferior quality. National mechanisms for quality control and standardization should be established or reinforced to encourage the development of products which are more reliable, better suited to local conditions and capable of inspiring greater public confidence.

The government could set an example in this respect through its procurement policy. To become a 'smart buyer', government administration must learn to set standards which will raise the performance level of domestic products. Acquisition of foreign technology should be negotiated so as to open the way for training of local personnel.

Special public offices could be created to suggest and implement policies in this respect. These offices could also play an advisory role for industry in all areas related to questions of intellectual property.

There is no scientific system for establishing priorities, even with respect to scientific and technological policies. And there is no certain way to ensure that, once they are designed, priorities will be implemented in an effective way. The two processes – establishment and implementation of priorities – are, in fact, intimately connected. Special mechanisms are needed to make the whole society, from government administrations to industry and trade unions, more aware of all the stakes inherent in these processes and more involved in the discussion of alternative policies.

In many cases – and all the more so in the case of S&T, which have not always been at the forefront of public debates in developing countries – a first stage of these efforts might fruitfully focus on making explicit hitherto implicit objectives of policies which have never been clearly formulated.

This process of elucidation might, in itself, serve as a powerful force in identifying the crucial stakeholders and bringing to light the most urgent steps to be taken.

Given the magnitude of present challenges for developing countries, we urge a new start in the management of the S&T base. This should begin with in-depth public discussions of the structures, processes, strengths, weaknesses and achievements of national S&T policies. These discussions should involve political parties, industrial and agricultural leaders and unions, scientists and engineers. Such debates are all the more necessary when policies have not been explicitly formulated in the past, in order to consider possible priorities and achieve a common sense of purpose among all participants.

In many countries, economic and social benefits which could be derived from the S&T base already established do not in fact meet expectations. This underlines the importance of the management of the scientific and technological system to adjust to new requirements. Managers in the public and industrial sectors have often not been adequately prepared for the new style of 'micro-management' which is called for at all stages, from the policy-making to the project level. The new style should blend decisiveness and risk-taking with flexibility and adjustment to the various concerns of the economic and social actors involved.

S&T policy already has a history and an accumulation of experience dating back many decades. There is no need to repeat costly mistakes which have already been made elsewhere, or to re-invent techniques and processes which have been already tested and refined. Policy-makers can thus draw enormous benefits from training in this area.

Special centres could be established to raise the S&T awareness of all decision-makers in all areas. In particular, the successful transfers of technology will often depend on the availability of informed intermediaries within the structure of different departments. These intermediaries will act as so many transfer points between the preoccupations of policy-makers and the expertise and concerns of the various other interest groups involved. The importance of these groups is such that it may well deserve special training efforts.

A limited number of high-quality centres for the training of S&T policy-makers and the study of S&T policy should be established regionally at institutions of higher education.

Special training sessions should be regularly offered to advanced students as well as to government officials and industrial and union leaders, among others. They should call upon foreign specialists when needed. Focusing on a special theme of particular relevance, these training sessions should be an opportunity to reach better understanding of local conditions and relevant traditional technological responses. They should also serve to establish contacts between professionals, future professionals, and scientists and engineers active in research or technical work. When undertaken regionally or internationally (which will often be the most effective solution) such recurrent sessions will provide a chance to compare experiences in different national contexts. These centres would provide a channel for transfer of experience and expertise to the less developed countries.

The very concept of development is not so much economic as political. It implies the mobilization of people to participate in decisions that affect their future well-being, as well as in the implementation of these decisions. This is particularly important in areas related to scientific and technological advances, which have a potentially enormous impact on life-styles, culture and economic traditions.

Much of what has been said above affects, directly or indirectly, the behaviour and participation of the various actors who have a stake in the progress of science and technology, ranging from researchers to policy-makers and industrialists, who could be referred to as 'stakeholders' in the innovation process.

Each of the groups involved must be aware of others who influence, directly or indirectly, the growth and application of scientific and technological efforts. These groups include scientists and engineers, academics, industrial leaders and managers, members of the public service, as well as policy-makers and politicians at national and subnational levels. It is only by ensuring intense and action-oriented interaction among all these groups that they will be turned into a community of 'stakeholders' in scientific and technological development, and will provide a basis to prevent discontinuities or disruptions which have compromised past efforts and threaten the future. Their support is particularly important for the development of scientific and technological institutions, and their involvement in the strategic management of these institutions crucial to safeguard their relevance to basic long-term problems of society and the economy.

The role of the stakeholders is equally important in preparing the way, at an early stage of research, for implementation of results.

The identification of 'stakeholders' who could become involved in the formulation of policies and their implementation should be attempted on a systematic basis. Assistance should be extended to the 'stakeholders' to help them organize themselves in an effective way, at international, national and local levels, through professional societies, clubs, associations, etc. They should be encouraged to develop joint projects to be submitted for consideration by government.

One of the major tasks of the managers of the S&T effort is to formulate strategies for the implementation of national priorities which will take account of the social, economic, scientific and technological dimensions of the problems at hand. For this purpose, countries need to develop a capacity to explore, develop and design policy options. Such a capacity implies that politicians and policy-makers are aware of the constraints and possibilities of scientific and technological research. It also implies that they have access to expert advice on the various dimensions of the problems. Advisory structures play a vital role in policy formulation and should be designed to reflect the broad range of relevant interests in the worlds of government, industry, science and technology, as well as society at large.

S&T policy can only be formulated in a comprehensive manner at the highest level of government. Each country will determine its own pattern in this respect (e.g. adviser to the Prime Minister, special ministry or agency, etc.), but in any case it will be necessary to provide for an advisory structure sufficiently broad to include representatives of all the major relevant concerns, sufficiently small to be effective, sufficiently close to the highest level of government to exercise influence on the choice of priorities and policies in all sectors, and sufficiently independent not to be constrained, in the advice given, by short-term considerations.

A major responsibility, for such advisory groups, should be to assess and clarify ecological implications of policies under consideration, and to suggest actions to prevent possible damage.

In a more general way, the evaluation and assessment of government policies can be an important contribution to policy debates, as an opportunity for clarification of impacts and achievements in the light of the many dimensions which should be taken into account (economic, social, cultural, ecological, etc.).

Evaluation of policy in all sectors should be promoted as a continuing activity, blended with the decision-making process itself. In many cases, and because of the small pool of expertise available nationally, evaluation and assessment could be undertaken on an international basis.

New approaches to industrialization

The so-called opportunity windows that developing countries are often invited to explore should not be understood as solely related to technological innovation and absorption. The new concepts of 'systemic flexible integration' and 'collective efficiency', when adequately developed and applied, may have enormous positive impacts in several areas of economic and cultural activities.

Industrial policies carried out in accordance with the Fordist paradigm are now becoming rapidly obsolete, with their emphasis on large-scale, rigid and standardized mass production based on economies of agglomeration, external economies and physical infrastructure. The new concept of 'flexible integration' introduces more advanced forms of productive organization, based on small, dynamic and flexible production units within an integrated system of continuous operation, involving suppliers of materials, components and services, who are linked by communications networks and thus able to respond rapidly to shifting consumer demands and markets with a great variety of high-quality and low-cost goods.

The very nature of such networks makes it impossible – and highly counter-productive – to attempt to orchestrate developments from above. Governments, however, have an important role to play here in assisting in the emergence of long-term strategies.

This type of assistance will include, for example, general orientation, guidance and support of industrial efforts, through the provision and discussion of analyses of opportunities, needs and potential economic dangers, based on informed intelligence (resulting from interpretation of foreign studies, data collection or technology assessment projects conducted at home).

One major goal should be to facilitate the emergence of a national consensus on medium- and long-term industrial targets, reflecting available scientific and technological resources. Government initiatives can go a long way here in establishing suitable locations and creating circumstances for indus-

124

trialists to meet with each other and to become acquainted with scientists and engineers.

The new forms of organization definitely offer opportunities for small and medium-sized firms to enter markets with relatively low initial investment in fixed capital (hardware), if the basic communications infrastructures are available and if they are able to call upon an existing potential of qualified human resources to adapt and/or develop the software required for flexible integration.

In many cases, the course to be followed to exploit such opportunities will tend to favour, as a first step, 'technological hybridization': local engineering capabilities and ingenuity can be called upon to update, upgrade or adapt old or imported capital goods. Maximum attention should also be devoted to the identification of opportunities for regional marketing of local production of goods and services.

As production becomes less based on raw materials and energy, and less labour-intensive, new forms of spatial organization become economically viable. Instead of large and inhuman metropolises, relatively small towns and cities may become alternative loci for the installation of production facilities, thus relieving the pressure on public spending for urban infrastructures and resulting in better quality of life. Within most medium-sized and large countries, such a process of industrial deconcentration will require sectorial and regional specialization.

Efforts should be made as a high priority of industrial policies to provide the basic infrastructure required for the networking of industry and services. While this effort could in itself offer an opportunity for the technological upgrading of small and medium-sized firms, it should also be accompanied by deliberate policies to encourage regional specialization.

In order to draw the maximum benefits from 'opportunity windows', several major policy changes will often prove necessary. As a rule, governments and development agencies should give priority to projects and programmes that pursue 'collective efficiency', instead of supporting isolated industrial projects.

Preference should be given to co-operative efforts involving small and/or medium-sized firms in close association with multidisciplinary assistance teams from universities and research centres. This strategy would represent a tremendous gain in overall effectiveness because it can multiply the benefits drawn from the scarce resources available in science and technology.

Once again, however, we emphasize the need for variation and diversification of guidelines for countries and regions which may now have vocations other than industrial. But one overriding condition will need to be met everywhere: the basic condition for development remains a solid and integrated domestic market, and S&T policies ought to be devised as one of the means to, and in conjunction with, structural changes based on sustainable growth in a context of social equity and in an open democratic society.

The contributions of international co-operation

One of the major deficiencies of international co-operation activities designed to support development has often been that they fail to adjust to the increasing heterogeneity of the developing world.

S&T development programmes must be designed to suit different groups of countries who have different needs. In particular, as countries acquire more diversified and advanced S&T resources, government aid may need to be increasingly complemented by non-governmental and industrial sources.

Special mechanisms need to be created to facilitate these new forms of co-operation and provide advice to the developing countries concerned in negotiating these new types of projects which will probably become more and more frequent.

Insufficient differentiation in the targets of S&T development co-operation has led to the relative neglect of the problems of those countries which have not yet acquired a domestic S&T infrastructure. This is an understandable trend: S&T programme managers will primarily turn to those that have an S&T base.

The future of the less-developed countries cannot be left entirely to depend on educational aid programmes which, as a rule, do not take into account the longer-term need to develop research capabilities. Affirmative action throughout the S&T aid programmes should be increased, in order to ensure that the requirements of science and engineering education, as well as of the future infrastructures needed for research, are fully taken into account.

Furthermore, and because they do not have an adequate S&T base, the least developed countries cannot address effectively many of their vital problems. Co-operative schemes developed to assist them in this connection should be systematically designed to contribute to the development of domestic S&T bases, for example, through the training of technical personnel.

We have already mentioned some of the key areas in which international co-operative schemes could provide needed aid: the collection of the basic data needed for sound development plans, the reinforcement of education, the exposure of developing countries to international scientific and technological life, and the evaluation of national programmes and research. The strategic goal is to provide support to establish the bases of endogenous scientific and technological resources.

The loss of qualified scientists, engineers and managers who emigrate to other countries may be one of the most disruptive factors in the generation of national S&T bases. The brain drain is a threat which reflects the inadequacy of the working conditions of highly qualified personnel in developing countries.

The efforts which must be made to keep or bring back these personnel certainly involve a realistic reappraisal of salaries and benefits of individuals in the light of national possibilities, but also – perhaps more importantly – the provision of state-of-the-art research facilities and equipment , the demonstration of the economic and social relevance of S&T work, and the creation of institutions and programmes designed to facilitate communication with colleagues abroad. The effectiveness of such measures will be greatly enhanced when undertaken at both national and regional levels, in co-ordination with international efforts.

In the light of what has been said about the need for diverse national approaches to account for different local conditions, there will be an increasing call on international co-operative schemes to provide linkages and information flows between various countries which focus in different ways on the same broad problem-areas of acute importance for several developing countries.

Regional centres should be strengthened, by co-operation with all international agencies involved in S&T aid for development, to provide training facilities, and meeting grounds for all S&T 'stakeholders'. These centres should in particular develop problem-oriented specializations which could serve to strengthen exchanges between different regions. In this framework, they should play a key role in extending support to policy research activities in developing countries, and in facilitating the diffusion of the results. One major role for these centres would be to systematically seek and explore opportunities for increased regional integration.

The agenda for policy research in developing countries is enormous, ranging from the implications of new socio-economic developments, such as urbanization, and the development of new industries, to a better under-standing of the challenge of blending new and traditional technologies, including evaluations of the effectiveness of various institutional and policy approaches to the solution of problems.

The diffusion of the results of this type of research is essential, because it stimulates policy changes and adjustments to take better account of the realities.

International programmes should do their utmost to stimulate policy research in developing countries. However, and because the stakes are very high, the diffusion of the results should be encouraged only when the research is of the highest quality. International experts should be called on to evaluate research designs, advise researchers during the implementation of projects, and pro-nounce on the scientific merits of the completed research.

In many instances, addressing local and regional problems will be greatly facilitated by co-operation between developing countries (not necessarily in the same regions) that face similar problems. One of the important roles the multilateral system of co-operation could play in this respect might be as a catalyst, identifying possible opportunities for co-operation and bringing together the actors concerned so that they can confront their respective strategies.

Most of the issues to be addressed may be relevant for a number of countries. International co-operation efforts can play an important role in confronting research approaches and conclusions, bringing together the scientists involved and disseminating the results, while continuing to build up a 'memory' of what has already been attempted and brought to light, so that the experience of the past can serve in future in different contexts.

S&T policy is an area where international experience, over the past decades, has been extremely rich and varied. Developing countries could benefit to a larger extent from the lessons to be drawn from the successes and failures of others.

Periodic surveys of the S&T scene and policies in countries could be underta-ken at international level. The potential value of such surveys, leading to pre-cise policy recommendations, will be realized only if the reviewers are fully independent experts.

Research priorities which shape the scientific and technological efforts of industrialized countries do not necessarily meet the needs of developing countries. This is because much of the research in question, often the most advanced and the most productive in terms of short-term application, is performed by industry (for example, in information and communications, biotechnologies and materials) and its priorities reflect the structure of international markets. There is often no 'solvent' market for products which are needed by developing countries – which is to say that the potential clients are too poor to represent an explicit demand. This situation will discourage industry from developing and marketing corresponding goods and services. In the pharmaceutical field, for example, the development and delivery of key medication may often have been delayed for these reasons until international public support provided a 'solvent' market .

Mechanisms should be developed to monitor the advances of worldwide research and identify areas where market forces fail to reflect the requirements of developing countries. New procedures and financial flows are needed to create, in such cases, solvent markets which will stimulate the application of scientific advances to attack major problems of developing countries, for example, with respect to health.

In this light, it would seem to be especially important to strengthen activities which serve as 'observatories' of scientific and technological progress to identify its potential relevance for developing countries and clarify economic and social implications. Such activities could be organized on a more systematic, worldwide basis.

This function could also serve as a basic framework for the continued monitoring of work under way in developing countries in order to disseminate information on progress and results. Special attention could be paid to the health and balance of key research institutions in developing countries which may be threatened by sudden disruption of their financial support, so that the international community can be alerted and take steps to prevent jeopardizing essential research resources that may be of great importance for entire regions.

New schemes must be found, however, to avoid excessive bureaucratization of co-operative schemes and ensure that he who pays does not directly attempt to organize the effort – a natural tendency which has brought about many failures in the past. The view of development which has been stressed above and which calls for the mobilization of all stakeholders in the definition of priorities and their implementation should be equally stressed at international level in order to prompt the creation of suitable mechanisms.

Finally, one special problem must be raised here relating to size. Very small developing countries cannot hope to address the broad range of scientific and technological issues by themselves. In such cases, international co-operation becomes a vital necessity to join forces with others and achieve critical mass in efforts in certain areas. Trained personnel, in such countries, is obviously a very scarce resource which should not lightly be diverted from productive activities to participate in endless administrative discussions. Administration should be integrated, as much as possible, into the normal operation of national projects. In this light, a 'pilot approach' – where a research institution in one country takes the lead to bring together physically, or to co-ordinate the work of, scientists from several other countries – is probably the most effective avenue to be explored in a number of research areas. The special asset of these countries is that, due to their small size, it is possible to multiply person-to-person relationships between scientists and engineers, and between them and industry, business and government circles.

At the other extreme, giant countries also have specific opportunities and difficulties to take into account. Today, China and India obviously belong to this category, but according to forecasts, at least fifteen developing countries will have passed the 100 million inhabitants mark in less than three decades. For these countries, a relatively small share of resources devoted to the S&T base can, in absolute terms, suffice to create a sizeable effort. As a result, it is possible to mobilize scientists and engineers to accomplish specific advanced technological objectives. However, it may be even more difficult than for others to develop the kind of networks between science, technology, the economy and society which is conducive to the blending of new and traditional technologies and to fruitful management of the S&T resources. Economic and social dualism thus entail not only risks of major disruptive upheavals, but also of overall lack of effectiveness in capitalizing on the opportunities offered by science and technology. For these countries, even more than for others, the goal of balanced development is essential and may call for relatively larger (rather than smaller) investments in science and technology.

Appendix

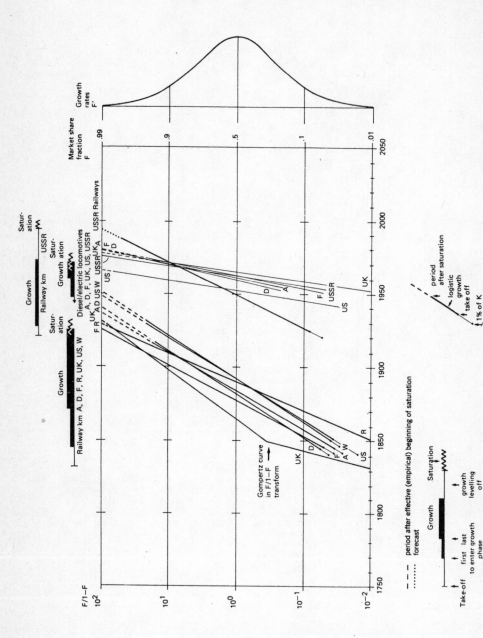

FIG. A1. Growth pulses in the expansion of the railway network and in the replacement of steam locomotives, as fractional growth

The dynamics of various expansion paths should be compared, leaving aside differences in absolute network size (which result from size of countries, geography, the location of main industrial and urban centres, etc.). The growth of railways in the industrial core countries is summarized using a logit model, whose most important feature is to allow consideration of each individual case within its own relevant boundary conditions: the growth of railways of a particular country is always compared in relation to the maximum network size (the saturation level of the growth process) attained in this same country

The model considers the fractional growth achieved, that is, the length of the railway network in any particular year divided by the ultimate maximum network size. This (comparable) measure brings to light a common pattern of the growth process of the development of railway infrastructures in different countries proceeding along a characteristic S-shaped diffusion trajectory, which can be mathematically approximated by a three-parameter logistic equation. In plotting the ratio of the fractional growth achieved over the growth potential remaining to be achieved (until reaching the maximum network size) on a logarithmic scale, the S-shaped growth patterns in the expansion of the railway networks of different countries become comparable as secular linear growth trends. The steeper the growth trajectory of a national railway network, the faster the growth process (see, for example, the catch-up effect in the development of the railway late-starter Russia). The discontinuous nature of this growth process is also highlighted in Figure 2 (Chapter 2), which illustrates the typical pattern of expansion rates of railway networks in all industrial core countries: slow growth rates at the beginning, and then increasing growth rates that reach a peak, finally to level off with the advent of saturation.

The diffusion of railways in industrial core countries took the form of an international diffusion bandwagon, with interconnected development trajectories due to their integration in terms of technology and capital transfers. This also applies to the subsequent transformations in the technology base of railways, as illustrated by the diffusion envelope of the substitution of (coal-powered) steam traction by diesel and electric traction in the railway sector of a number of countries. Thus, the substitution of steam by diesel/electric locomotives proceeds with a similar dynamic (logistic) trajectory in all countries analysed, independent of their economic system, that is, a type of diffusion bandwagon characteristic of the evolution of the technological base of a mature technological system.

The existence of international diffusion bandwagons highlights the importance of integration into international flows of technology, capital and skills. Opportunity windows for participating in the development of a particular technological cluster at the international level may thus exist only during limited time periods.

At a later stage, the diffusion and intensity levels achieved by the core countries of a particular bandwagon no longer serve as development models. Desirable development levels for particular technology clusters cannot therefore be defined through a normative framework based on the experience of countries which started earlier.

TABLE A1. Distribution of countries according to population (mid 1987)

Country	Population (millions)
1. Very very small	
Seychelles	0.10
Sao Tomé and Principe	0.10
Dominique	0.10
Grenada	0.10
Maldives	0.20
Brunei	0.20
Samoa	0.20
Belize	0.20
Bahamas	0.20
Iceland	0.20
Barbados	0.30
Cape Verde	0.30
Qatar	0.30
Solomon Islands	0.30
Djibouti	0.40
Equatorial Guinea	0.41
Bahrain	0.40
Macao	0.40
Suriname	0.40
Luxembourg	0.40
Malta	0.40
Comoros	0.50
Swaziland	0.70
Cyprus	0.70
Timor	0.70
Fiji	0.70
Zambia	0.80
Guinea-Bissau	0.90
Guyana	1.00
Mauritius	1.00
Gabon	1.10
Botswana	1.20
Trinidad and Tobago	1.20
Oman	1.30
Namibia	1.70
2. Very small	
United Arab Emirates	1.40
Bhutan	1.40

Country	Population (millions)
Lesotho	1.60
Liberia	1.60
Congo	1.80
Kuwait	1.90
Mauritania	1.90
Mongolia	2.00
Panama	2.30
Yemen (Republic of)	2.40
Jamaica	2.50
Singapore	2.60
Central African Republic	2.70
Costa Rica	2.80
Lebanon	2.80
Uruguay	3.00
Albania	3.10
Togo	3.10
New Zealand	3.30
Nicaragua	3.50
Ireland	3.50
Papua New Guinea	3.50
Jordan	3.80
Laos	3.80
Paraguay	3.90
Sierra Leone	3.90
Libyan Arab Jamahiriya	4.10
Norway	4.20
Benin	4.30
Israel	4.40
Honduras	4.70
Finland	4.90
Chad	5.30

3. Small

Burundi	5.00
Salvador	5.00
Guinea	5.00
Denmark	5.10
Hong Kong	5.40
Haiti	6.20
Yemen (Dem.)	6.50
Cambodia	6.50
Rwanda	6.50

TABLE A1 – *continued*

Country	Population (millions)
Niger	6.50
Switzerland	6.60
Dominican Republic	6.70
Bolivia	6.80
Senegal	6.90
Zambia	7.10
Malawi	7.50
Tunisia	7.60
Austria	7.60
Somali	7.70
Angola	8.00
Burkina Faso	8.30
Zimbabwe	8.60
Mali	8.70
Guatemala	8.40
Sweden	8.40
Bulgaria	9.00
Belgium	9.90

4. *Medium-size*

Country	Population (millions)
Ecuador	10.00
Greece	10.00
Cuba	10.30
Portugal	10.30
Hungary	10.60
Cameroon	10.80
Madagascar	10.90
Syrian Arab Republic	11.00
Côte d'Ivoire	11.10
Chile	12.50
Ghana	13.40
Saudi Arabia	13.60
Mozambique	14.50
Netherlands	14.60
Afghanistan	15.20
Czechoslovakia	15.60
Malaysia	16.10
Australia	16.20
Sri Lanka	16.40
Uganda	16.60
Germany (GDR)	16.70
Iraq	17.00

Country	Population (millions)
Nepal	17.80
Venezuela	18.30
Taiwan	19.60
Peru	20.70
Korea (Dem.)	21.40
Kenya	22.90
Romania	22.90
Algeria	23.00
Sudan	23.10
United Republic of Tanzania	23.20
Morocco	23.30
Yugoslavia	23.40
Canada	25.60
Colombia	29.70

5. *Large*

Argentina	31.50
Zaire	32.50
South Africa	33.00
Poland	37.80
Myanmar	38.80
Spain	39.00
Korea (Republic of)	41.60
Ethiopia	46.20
Islamic Republic of Iran	50.40
Egypt	50.70
Turkey	51.30
Thailand	53.60
France	55.60
United Kingdom	56.80
Italy	57.40
Philippines	57.40
Germany (Federal Republic of)	61.00
Viet Nam	62.80
Mexico	81.20
Nigeria	101.90
Pakistan	102.20
Bangladesh	102.60
Japan	122.10
Brazil	141.50
Indonesia	170.20
United States	243.90

TABLE A1 – *continued*

Country	Population (millions)
USSR	283.00
6. *Very large*	
India	781.40
China	1089.00

Source: United Nations, *Demographic Yearbook 1988*, Table 5 pp. 185–9.

TABLE A2. Gross domestic product per capita (1985) (in US dollars)

Country	per capita GDP
Group I: Low-income	
Ethiopia	187
Chad	193
United Republic of Tanzania	280
Burkina Faso	283
Mali	296
Zaire	300
Bhutan	311
Niger	351
Burundi	354
Malawi	355
Guinea-Bissau	359
Mozambique	385
Bangladesh	398
Rwanda	399
Lesotho	402
Nepal	405
Central African Republic	414
Uganda	415
Zambia	437
Sierra Leone	439
Madagascar	444
Cape Verde	445
Benin	448
Somali	479
Togo	486
Guinea	530
Sao Tomé and Principe	547
Kenya	548
Myanmar	579

Country	per capita GDP
India	582
Sudan	589
Afghanistan	590
Group II: Lower middle-income	
Angola	600
Equatorial Guinea	614
Nigeria	621
Ghana	648
Senegal	657
Liberia	692
Mauritania	706
Yemen (Dem.)	756
Maldives	846
Zimbabwe	857
Yemen (Republic of)	884
Cameroon	943
Côte d'Ivoire	959
Honduras	992
China	1 010
Pakistan	1 013
Bolivia	1 020
Swaziland	1 024
El Salvador	1 040
Guyana	1 112
Indonesia	1 131
Morocco	1 197
Djibouti	1 234
SriLanka	1 268
Egypt	1 348
Philippines	1 409
Grenada	1 435
Mauritius	1 536
Nicaragua	1 577
Group III: Middle middle-income	
Congo	1 603
Solomon Islands	1 611
Papua New Guinea	1 676
Dominique	1 722
Belize	1 773
Dominican Rep	1 781
Samoa	1 783

Table A2 – *continued*

Country	per capita GDP
Cuba	1 857
Guatemala	1 859
Botswana	1 903
Thailand	1 942
Tunisia	2 008
Paraguay	2 065
Peru	2 111
Jordan	2 116
Jamaica	2 175
Iraq	2 211
Seychelles	2 270
Ecuador	2 271
Algeria	2 313
Lebanon	2 316
Colombia	2 595
Costa Rica	2 603
Syrian Arab Republic	2 609
Turkey	2 675
Argentina	2 980
Brazil	3 031
Chile	3 053
Panama	3 187
Islamic Republic of Iran	3 187
Uruguay	3 217
Korea (Republic of)	3 275
Malaysia	3 309
South Africa	3 357
Fiji	3 406
Barbados	3 544
Mexico	3 597
Venezuela	3 819
Yugoslavia	4 036
Romania	4 156
Portugal	4 272
Haiti	4 286
Poland	4 358
Malta	4 462
Gabon	4 531
Greece	4 639
Trinidad and Tobago	4 698
Taiwan	4 733
Bulgaria	4 750
Cyprus	4 929

Country	per capita GDP
Hungary	5 231
USSR	5 281
Ireland	5 531
Czechoslovakia	5 812
Bahamas	6 063
Spain	6 313
Germany (GDR)	6 384
Libyan Arab Jamahiriya	6 395
Israel	6 532
New Zealand	7 216
Oman	7 266
Italy	7 532
Saudi Arabia	7 976
Group IV: Upper-income	
Hong Kong	8 333
Singapore	8 347
Austria	8 564
United Kingdom	8 845
Kuwait	8 884
Belgium	8 953
France	8 991
Netherlands	8 998
Finland	9 157
Brunei	9 198
Japan	9 435
Australia	9 447
Bahrain	9 507
Iceland	9 592
Denmark	9 958
Germany (Federal Republic of)	9 977
Luxembourg	10 625
Sweden	11 012
Switzerland	11 626
Norway	11 700
Canada	12 060
United States	12 467
United Arab Emirates	13 096
Qatar	14 995

Note: Countries exporting more than 0.5 per cent of total world exports of a commodity are printed in italics.

Source: World Bank, *World Development Report 1988*, Table 2 for GDP data.

TABLE A3. Major developing-country exporters of manufactured products (1985 or latest available)

Country	Total national exports (%)	Total manufactured exports of developing countries (%)
Taiwan	93.1	26.6
Korea	83.4	23.2
Hong Kong	95.3	15.4
Singapore	48.2	12.0
Brazil	31.9	7.9
Mexico	12.8	3.2
Argentina	13.9	1.2
TOTAL		89.5

Source: J. W. Sewell, S. K. Tucker, et al., *Growth, Exports and Jobs in a Changing World Economy,* New Brunswick, N.J./Oxford, Transaction Books, 1988.

TABLE A4. Heterogeneity of very very small countries per million inhabitants (1985 or latest available)

Country	Population	GDP per head (US dollars)
Seychelles	0.10	2 270
Sao Tomé and Principe	0.10	547
Dominique	0.10	1 722
Grenada	0.10	1 435
Maldives	0.20	846
Brunei	0.20	9 198
Samoa	0.20	1 783
Belize	0.20	1 773
Bahamas	0.20	6 063
Iceland	0.20	9 592
Cape Verde	0.30	445
Qatar	0.30	14 995
Solomon Islands	0.30	1 611
Barbados	0.30	3 544
Djibouti	0.40	1 234
Equatorial Guinea	0.40	614
Bahrain	0.40	9 507
Macao	0.40	
Suriname	0.40	

Country	Population	GDP per head (US dollars)
Luxembourg	0.40	10 625
Malta	0.40	4 462
Comoros	0.50	
Swaziland	0.70	1 024
Cyprus	0.70	4 929
Timor	0.70	
Fiji	0.70	3 406
Gambia	0.80	437
Guyana	1.00	1 112 ·
Mauritius	1.00	1536
Gabon	1.20	4 531
Botswana	1.20	1 903
Trinidad and Tobago	1.20	4 698
Oman	1.30	7 266
Namibia	1.70	
Guinea-Bissau	2.00	359

Sources: United Nations, *Demographic Yearbook 1988*, Table 5 pp. 185–9; World Bank, *World Development Report 1988*, Table 2, for GDP data.

TABLE A5. Percentage of GNP devoted to R&D (1986 or latest available)

Country	R&D share of GNP
Group I	
Congo	0.0
Jamaica	0.0
Malta	0.0
Brunei-Darussalam	0.1
Colombia	0.1
Cyprus	0.1
Niger	0.1
Central African Republic	0.2
Egypt	0.2
Greece	0.2
Guyana	0.2
Jordan	0.2
Libyan Arab Jamahirya	0.2
Madagascar	0.2
Malawi	0.2
Panama	0.2

TABLE A5 – *continued*

Country	R&D share of GNP
Peru	0.2
Philippines	0.2
Rwanda	0.2
Sri Lanka	0.2
Sudan	0.2
Turkey	0.2
Costa Rica	0.3
Fiji	0.3
Indonesia	0.3
Mauritius	0.3
Nicaragua	0.3
Nigeria	0.3
Pakistan	0.3
Thailand	0.3
Group II	
Argentina	0.4
Burundi	0.4
Ecuador	0.4
Portugal	0.4
Venezuela	0.4
Group III	
Chile	0.5
Guatemala	0.5
Singapore	0.5
Spain	0.5
Mexico	0.6
Brazil	0.7
Cuba	0.8
Iceland	0.8
Trinidad and Tobago	0.8
Yugoslavia	0.8
India	0.9
Ireland	0.9
Kuwait	0.9
New Zealand	0.9
Senegal	1.0
Austria	1.2
Poland	1.2
Group IV	
Australia	1.3
Denmark	1.3

Country	R&D share of GNP
Italy	1.3
Seychelles	1.3
Belgium	1.4
Canada	1.5
Finland	1.5
El Salvador	1.7
Korea (Dem)	1.8
Norway	1.9
Netherlands	2.1
Switzerland	2.2
United Kingdom	2.2
France	2.3
Germany (Federal Republic of)	2.5
Israel	2.5
Hungary	2.6
Japan	2.8
United States	2.8
Sweden	3.0
Bulgaria	3.2
Czechoslovakia	4.1
Germany (GDR)	4.5
USSR	5.1

Note: Net material product for Bulgaria, Czechoslovakia, Poland and USSR; global social product for Cuba.

Source: UNESCO, *Statistical Yearnook 1988,* Table 5.19.

TABLE A6. Scientists and engineers engaged in R&D per million inhabitants[1] (1985 or latest available). Data are expressed in full-time equivalents

Country	Scientists and engineers
Group I	
Jamaica	8
Rwanda (1978)	12
Madagascar	13
Niger	19
Nepal	23
Kenya	26
Nigeria (1977)	30
Malawi	35
Colombia	40
Burundi	48

TABLE A6 – *continued*

Country	Scientists and engineers
Zambia	50
Fiji (1976)	51
Myanmar	57
Lebanon	67
Islamic Republic of Iran (1982)	72
Côte d'Ivoire	74
Cyprus	77
Jordan (1977)	77
Central African Republic	78
Malta	88
Brunei-Darussalam (1981)	90
Pakistan	91
Guyana (1980)	99
Group II	
Senegal	106
Togo	113
Philippines (1980)	117
Panama (1975)	121
India	134
Turkey (1980)	163
Sri Lanka	172
Indonesia (1980)	175
Malaysia (1982)	182
Nicaragua	199
Guinea	216
Mexico	216
Sudan	217
Trinidad and Tobago	235
Paraguay	247
Group III	
Greece (1981)	250
Seychelles	250
Brazil (1980)	256
Ecuador	259
Peru	273
Venezuela (1982)	279
Mauritius (1983)	285
Viet Nam	335
Portugal	342
Guatemala	348
Argentina (1980)	360
Libyan Arab Jamahiriya	370
Ghana	403

Country	Scientists and engineers
Spain (1984)	421
Chile	422
Egypt	435
Congo (1977)	509
Qatar (1983)	702
El Salvador	807
Kuwait (1980)	887
Austria	894
Samoa (1977)	909
Singapore (1980)	949
Cuba (1981)	991
Group IV	
Ireland (1981)	1 016
Italy (1981)	1 113
Korea (Republic of) (1981)	1 120
Poland (1984)	1 210
Yugoslavia (1981)	1 317
Iceland (1975)	1 345
Belgium	1 414
Canada (1981)	1 489
United Kingdom	1 545
Denmark (1980)	1 673
Australia (1982)	1 862
France	1 873
Switzerland (1980)	2 101
Hungary (1984)	2 152
Germany (Federal Republic of) (1980)	2 178
Netherlands	2 319
Norway	2 439
Sweden (1979)	2 539
New Zealand	2 558
United States (1982)	3 282
Czechoslovakia (1980)	4 019
Japan (1982)	4 743
Bulgaria (1983)	5 094
USSR	5 351
Germany (GDR)	7 816
Israel	9 525

1. Scientists and engineers: those with S&T training (usually completion of third-level education) and engaged in professional work on R&D activities, administrators or other high-level personnel who direct the execution of R&D activities.

Source: UNESCO, *Statistical Yearbook 1988,* Table 5.18.

Table A7. R&D personnel in higher education per thousand inhabitants (1985 or latest available). Data are expressed in full-time equivalents

Country	R&D personnel
Group I	
Burundi	0.01
Kenya	0.01
Niger	0.01
Rwanda	0.01
Cyprus	0.03
India	0.03
Malawi	0.03
Philippines[1]	0.03
Zambia	0.03
Colombia	0.05
Pakistan[2]	0.05
Central African Republic	0.06
Lebanon	0.06
Togo	0.06
Jordan	0.07
Chile	0.09
Costa Rica	0.09
El Salvador	0.09
Nicaragua[3]	0.09
Sri Lanka	0.09
Group II	
Viet Nam	0.10
Argentina	0.11
Brazil	0.11
Panama	0.11
Ecuador	0.12
Guinea	0.12
Malta	0.12
Greece	0.14
Turkey	0.14
Sudan	0.15
Mauritius	0.17
Guyana[4]	0.19
Group III	
Libyan Arab Jamahiriya	0.21
Spain	0.22
Kuwait[3]	0.24
Trinidad and Tobago	0.24
Congo[3]	0.25

Country	R&D personnel
Portugal	0.27
Peru	0.28
Cuba	0.32
Venezuela[3]	0.32
Mexico	0.33
Czechoslovakia	0.35
Group IV	
Poland	0.42
New Zealand	0.43
Samoa	0.43
Egypt	0.46
United States[2]	0.46
Canada	0.56
Austria	0.63
Italy	0.64
Ireland	0.65
Korea (Republic of)[2, 3]	0.68
Hungary	0.74
Singapore[3]	0.76
Qatar[2]	0.80
Belgium	0.84
Denmark	0.90
Yugoslavia	1.00
Iceland	1.01
France	1.06
Switzerland	1.06
Netherlands	1.11
Finland	1.20
Germany (Federal Republic of)	1.21
Australia	1.24
Norway	1.27
Sweden	1.69
Japan	1.94

1. Part-time scientists and engineers not accounted for.
2. Social sciences and humanities not included.
3. Addition of full-time and part-time scientists and engineers.
4. Medical sciences not included.

Source: UNESCO, *Statistical Yearbook 1988,* Table 5.6.

TABLE A8. Third-level students per 100,000 inhabitants (1985 or latest available)

Country	Number of students
Group I	
Mozambique	10
Bhutan	17
United Republic of Tanzania	26
Rwanda	33
Chad	34
Niger	48
Angola	53
Burkina Faso	57
Burundi	59
Malawi	59
Ethiopia	63
Uganda	65
Yemen (Republic of)	76
Mali	81
Haiti	101
Central African Republic	103
Kenya	106
Guinea	109
Mauritius	119
Ghana	125
Zambia	128
Afghanistan	129
Lao	131
Zaire	137
Togo	156
Lesotho	158
Oman	168
Sudan	173
Botswana	175
Yemen (Republic of)	177
Papua New Guinea	178
Benin	179
China	184
Cameroon	185
Group II	
Côte d'Ivoire	208
Senegal	209
Viet Nam	212
Luxembourg	232
Nigeria	239

Country	Number of students
Guyana	244
Mauritania	248
Fiji	314
Swaziland	328
Somalia	330
Gabon	349
Sri Lanka	364
Malta	377
Madagascar	383
Nepal	397
Bangladesh	445
Trinidad and Tobago	464
Islamic Republic of Iran	478
Pakistan	487
Myanmar	489
Jamaica	508
Tunisia	564
Congo	572
Malaysia	599
Indonesia	600
United Arab Emirates	603
Cyprus	621
Algeria[2]	690
Romania	694
Albania	719
India	744
Guatemala	755
Nicaragua	791
Morocco	820
Libyan Arab Jamahirya	832
Honduras	838
Iraq	856
Suriname	890
Group III	
Hungary	923
Paraguay	929
Bahrain	967
Turkey	1 003
Czechoslovakia	1 088
Saudi Arabia	1 097
Portugal	1 112
Brazil	1 140
Poland	1 205

TABLE A8 – *continued*

Country	Number of students
El Salvador	1 292
Kuwait	1 307
Bulgaria	1 381
Singapore	1 406
Hong Kong	1 410
Colombia	1 423
Mexico	1 508
Yugoslavia	1 509
Qatar	1 619
Chile	1 640
Bolivia	1 648
Syrian Arab Republic	1 665
Group IV	
Greece	1 709
Switzerland	1 789
United Kingdom	1 806
USSR	1 814
Ireland	1 888
Egypt[1]	1 918
Dominican Republic	1 982
Japan	1 987
Italy	1 989
Mongolia	1 991
Jordan	1 992
Thailand	1 998
Iceland	2 040
Barbados	2 065
Norway	2 124
Denmark	2 271
Peru	2 339
France[3]	2 358
Austria	2 398
Australia	2 453
Costa Rica	2 498
Cuba	2 526
Belgium	2 546
Germany (Federal Republic of)	2 546
Venezuela	2 559
Germany (GDR)	2 608
Spain	2 626
Lebanon	2 634
Sweden	2 635

Country	Number of students
Finland	2 733
Israel	2 746
Panama	2 787
Netherlands	2 792
Argentina	2 911
New Zealand	3 066
Ecuador	3 078
Uruguay	3 357
Korea (Republic of)	3 606
Philippines	3 621
Canada	4 853
United States	5 167

Note: programmes taken into account: only those which lead to recognized third-level degrees, including evening and correspondence courses.
1. Not including female students in private institutions.
2. Female students not included.
3. Overestimate due to double enrolments.

Source: UNESCO, *Statistical Yearbook 1988*, Table 3.6.

TABLE A9. Potential scientists and engineers (latest figures available)[1]

Country	Number
Group I	
Djibouti (1973)	35
Solomon Islands (1971)	129
Dominica (1970)	162
Grenada (1970)	233
Fiji (1976)	305
Samoa (1977)	350
Belize (1970)	419
Togo (1971)	461
Botswana (1972)[2]	786
Seychelles (1983)[2]	900
Barbados (1970)	1 163
Swaziland (1971)[2]	1 384
Yemen (Republic of) (1974)	1 394
Guyana (1980)	1 512
Rwanda (1978)	1 762
Mongolia (1972)	1 908

TABLE A9 – *continued*

Country	Number
Brunei-Darussalam (1981)[2]	2 214
Papua New Guinea 1973)[2]	2 646
Bahamas (1970)	3 000
Trinidad and Tobago1970)	3 314
Tunisia (1974)[5]	3 421
Nepal (1980)[7]	3 668
Malawi (1977)[4]	3 981
Iceland 1975)	5 024
Panama (1976)	5 415
El Salvador (1974)	5 489
Guatemala (1974)	5 551
Jamaica (1970)	5 963
Qatar (1983)[2]	6 302
Honduras (1974)	6 702
Ghana (1970)[2]	6 897
Mauritius (1983)	7 256
Sri Lanka (1972)	7 457
Dominican Republic(1970) [4]	7 837
Sudan (1971)	9 708
Bahrain (1981)[2]	10 747
Zambia (1973)	11 000
Jordan (1977)	11 575
Cameroon (1976)[3]	11 785
Haiti (1982)[6]	14 189
Kenya (1982)	16 241
Myanmar (1975)[7]	18 500
Group II	
Thailand (1975)[7]	20 288
Nigeria (1980)	22 050
Bengladesh (1973)	23 500
Syrian Arab Republic (1970)	24 523
Malaysia (1982)[7]	26 000
Lebanon (1972)[6]	28 530
Saudi Arabia (1974)	33 376
Singapore (1980)	38 259
Iraq (1972)[10]	43 645
Libyan Arab Jamahiriya (1980)[2]	43 737
New Zealand (1971)	47 249
Ecuador (1974)	48 559
Uruguay (1975)[4]	56 400
Bolivia (1976)[8]	58 090
Chile (1970)[4]	69 946

Country	Number
Kuwait (1980)[2]	78 795
Group III	
Denmark (1980)	83 529
Korea (Republic of) (1981)	94 171
Pakistan (1973)[7]	100 500
Norway (1985)	114 830
Cuba (1981)	139 469
Hong Kong (1986)	145 523
Austria (1981)	153 923
Israel (1984)	174 518
Finland (1984)	183 870
Indonesia (1980)	193 262
Peru (1981)	291 812
Islamic Republic of Iran (1982)	294 647
Bulgaria (1983)	302 809
Greece (1981)	329 489
Sweden (1979)	335 900
Venezuela (1982)	347 000
Switzerland (1980) [4]	348 167
Australia (1981)	383 368
Yugoslavia (1981)	460 688
Hungary (1984)	487 300
Group IV	
Egypt (1976)[4]	492 470
Argentina (1980)	535 656
Czechoslovakia (1980)[3]	542 706
Germany (GDR) (1986)	600 000
Turkey (1980)[6]	708 000
Ireland (1981)	831 790
Netherlands (1985)	972 300
Italy (1981)	1 175 418
Spain (1984)	1 182 500
France (1975)	1 251 610
Canada (1981)	1 291 210
Brazil (1980)	1 362 206
Poland (1984)	1 423 000
Philippines (1980)	1 758 614
Germany (Federal Republic of) (1980)	2 278 000
India* (1985)[7]	2 560 800
United States (1982) (6)	3 431 800
Japan (1982)	7 046 000

TABLE A9 – *continued*

Country	Number
China* (1984) (6) (8)	7 466 000
USSR (1986)	15 000 000

1. The number of individuals who possess the necessary qualifications to become scientists and engineers.
2. Including foreigners.
3. Persons aged 15 and over.
4. Persons aged 25 and over.
5. Data underestimated.
6. Based on sample survey.
7. Social Sciences and Humanities not included.
8. Persons aged 20 and over.
9. Not including data for collective organisations.
10. Public employees only.

Source: UNESCO, *Statistical Yearbook 1988*, Table 5.3.

TABLE A10. R&D personnel in industry as a percentage of total R&D personnel, 1985 or latest year available

Country	
Group A	
Chile (1984)	1.5
Colombia (1982)	2.6
Mauritius (1986)	2.8
Greece (1979)	3.0
Cuba (1986)[1]	3.7
Argentina (1982)	4.5
Ecuador (1979)	5.1
Egypt (1986)	5.8
Philippines (1982)	5.9
Iceland (1979)	6.7
Jordan (1985)	6.7
Sri Lanka (1985)	7.1
Costa Rica (1982)	7.9
Group B	
Venezuela (1983)	8.4
Turkey (1983)	9.1
Peru (1981)	9.7
Kenya (1975)	11.2
Kuwait (1984)	11.7
Rwanda (1985)	12.6
Portugal (1984)	16.9

Country	
Libyan Arab Jamahiriya (1980)	18.2
Poland (1986)	19.2
India (1984)	21.5
New Zealand (1979)[2]	22.9
Guinea (1984)	23.8
Group C	
Australia (1985)	24.5
Samoa (1978)	26.1
Yugoslavia (1986)[1]	26.7
Trinidad and Tobago (1984)	26.9
Ireland (1984)[2]	29.1
Congo (1984)[1]	33.8
Singapore (1984)	34.0
Sudan (1978)	35.0
Mexico (1984)	35.2
Czechoslovakia (1986)	37.0
Norway (1986)	38.9
Malawi (1977)	39.4
Italy (1985)	47.7
Netherlands (1985)	48.0
Spain (1985)[2]	48.2
Zambia (1976)	48.4
Hungary (1986)	48.8
Korea (Republic of) (1986)[1]	48.8
Finland (1985)	50.0
Denmark (1985)	50.4
France (1985)[2]	51.5
Austria (1981)	55.0
Bulgaria (1986)	56.6
Japan (1986)	59.3
El Salvador (1981)	65.3
Germany (Federal Republic of) (1983)	66.8
Viet Nam (1985)	69.0
United Kingdom (1978)	70.5
United States (1986)	73.7
Pakistan (1986)[1]	73.9
Guyana (1982)[1]	75.3
Switzerland (1979)	75.6
Nicaragua (1985)	79.3

1. Military and defence not included.
2. Including services.

Source: UNESCO, *Statistical Yearbook 1988,* Table 5.6.

TABLE A11. Percentage of manufacturing in GDP (1986)

Countries	Share of GDP	Group
Guinea	2	B
Benin	4	A
Central African Republic	4	A
Niger	4	A
Sierra Leone	4	A
Liberia	5	A
Uganda	5	A
Botswana	6	A
Congo	6	C
Somalia	6	A
United Republic of Tanzania	6	
Mali	7	A
Sudan	7	C
Togo	7	B
Yemen (Republic of)	7	A
Bangladesh	8	A
Nigeria	8	B
Panama	8	C
Trinidad and Tobago	8	C
Papua New Guinea	9	A
Saudi Arabia	9	B
Myanmar	10	A
Burundi	10	A
Ethiopia	10	A
Ghana	12	B
Kenya	12	A
Malawi	12	B
Algeria	13	B
Bolivia	13	B
Lesotho	13	A
Honduras	14	A
Indonesia	14	B
Jordan	14	C
Norway	14	D
El Salvador	15	C
Sri Lanka	15	B
Tunisia	15	B
Dominican Republic	16	B
Côte d'Ivoire	16	
Paraguay	16	B
Rwanda	16	A
Australia	17	D

Countries	Share of GDP	Group
Morocco	17	
Pakistan	17	C
Senegal	17	B
Colombia	18	C
Greece	18	C
Netherlands	18	D
Ecuador	19	C
India	19	C
Denmark	20	D
Peru	20	C
United States	20	D
Zambia	20	B
Thailand	21	C
Italy	22	D
Jamaica	22	B
South Africa	22	
Belgium	23	D
Mauritius	23	C
Venezuela	23	C
Sweden	24	D
Finland	25	C
Philippines	25	C
Turkey	25	C
Mexico	26	C
United Kingdom	26	D
Hong Kong	27	C
Nicaragua	27	C
Singapore	27	C
Spain	27	D
Austria	28	D
Brazil	28	C
Japan	30	D
Korea (Republic of)	30	C
Zimbabwe	30	A
Afghanistan	31	B
Germany (Federal Republic of)	32	D
China	34	B

Source: World Bank, *World Development Report 1988,* Table 3.

TABLE A12. Growth of manufacturing value added (MVA) (1980–86)

Countries	MVA	Group
Trinidad and Tobago	−12.8	C
Bolivia	−9.0	B
Liberia	−5.0	A
United Republic of Tanzania	−4.6	
Somalia	−3.4	A
Togo	−2.6	A
Haiti	−2.6	A
Honduras	−2.1	A
Ghana	−1.9	B
South Africa	−1.7	
Philippines	−1.7	C
Guatemala	−1.6	C
El Salvador	−1.1	C
Zaire	−0.7	A
Central African Republic	−0.6	A
Argentina	−0.4	C
Uganda	−0.3	A
Italy	−0.2	D
Chile	−0.2	C
Sudan	0.0	A
Mexico	0.0	C
Panama	0.2	C
Greece	0.2	C
Norway	0.3	D
Spain	0.3	D
Dominican Republic	0.4	B
Paraguay	0.5	B
Zambia	0.6	A
Nicaragua	0.8	B
Germany (Federal Republic of)	0.8	D
Nigeria	1.0	B
Jamaica	1.1	B
United Kingdom	1.2	D
Brazil	1.2	C
Zimbabwe	1.3	A
Guinea	1.5	A
Belgium	1.6	D
Sierra Leone	2.0	A
Venezuela	2.0	C
Bangladesh	2.1	A
Austria	2.1	D
Singapore	2.2	C

Countries	MVA	Group
Sweden	2.3	D
Colombia	2.5	B
Congo	2.9	B
Denmark	2.9	D
Finland	3.0	C
Canada	3.6	D
Ethiopia	3.8	A
United States	4.0	D
Kenya	4.1	A
Rwanda	4.1	A
Senegal	4.1	B
Benin	4.6	A
Jordan	4.9	B
Thailand	5.2	C
Sri Lanka	5.6	B
Myanmar	5.8	A
Malaysia	5.8	B
Saudi Arabia	6.1	B
Botswana	6.2	A
Tunisia	6.5	B
Burundi	6.9	A
Indonesia	7.7	B
Mauritius	7.8	B
Japan	7.8	D
Turkey	8.0	C
India	8.2	C
Pakistan	9.3	B
Korea (Republic of)	9.8	C
Morocco	11.0	
China	12.6	B
Lesotho	16.1	A

Source: World Bank, *World Development Report 1988*, Table 2.

TABLE A13. Percentage of GNP devoted to third-level education (1975–86)

Country	1975	1980	1982	1983	1984	1985	1986	Group
Angola				5.5	5.0	5.2		A
Argentina	2.5	3.6		2.8		2.2	1.8	C
Bahrain[1]		2.8		3.2	3.5	3.8	5.0	B
Bangladesh[23]		1.5		1.8	1.8	1.9	2.1	A
Bolivia				2.7	5.0			B

TABLE A13 – *continued*

Country	1975	1980	1982	1983	1984	1985	1986	Group
Botswana	8.5	7.1		7.5	8.2	7.7	6.0	A
Brazil	3.0	3.5	4.6	3.3	2.8	3.3		C
Burkina Faso		2.6		3.1	2.8	2.7	2.5	A
Cameroon	3.9	3.2		3.5	3.2	3.8		A
Canada	7.6	7.4		7.7	7.2	7.0	7.4	D
Chile[1]	4.1	4.6	5.7	5.0	4.8	4.5		C
China	1.8	2.5		2.7	2.6	2.7		B
Colombia[12]	2.2	1.9		2.9	3.2	2.9	2.9	B
Congo	8.1	6.9	5.4	5.8	4.9			B
Costa Rica	6.8	7.8		5.6	6.0	4.7	5.2	B
Cuba	5.7	7.2	6.3	5.9	6.4	6.3		C
Dominican Republic[2]		2.3		2.3	2.0	1.8	1.6	B
Ecuador		5.6		3.8	4.1	3.6	3.4	C
Egypt	5.1		5.5					C
Gabon	2.1	2.8			4.1	4.5		B
Guatemala	1.6		1.9	1.8	1.8			C
Honduras	3.7	3.3	4.3			4.6	5.0	A
Hong Kong	2.7	2.5	2.9	2.8	2.8			C
India[3]	2.8	3.0	3.1	3.4	3.7	3.6		C
Indonesia	2.7	1.7						B
Iraq[1]		2.6	4.2	4.1	3.9	3.8		B
Jamaica				7.5	6.5	5.8		B
Japan[4]	5.5	5.8	5.6	5.6	5.2	5.1		D
Jordan		6.5		6.3	8.0	7.1		B
Kenya[2]	6.3	6.9	6.6	5.1	5.8	6.7		A
Korea (Republic of)	2.2	3.7		5.0	4.8	4.8	4.5	C
Madagascar	3.2	5.4	4.0	3.4	3.8	3.5		A
Malawi	2.4	3.3	3.0	2.8	2.6	3.3		A
Malaysia	6.0	6.0	7.4		6.1	6.6	7.8	B
Mali[5]		3.6	3.5		3.3	3.5	2.8	A
Mauritius	3.6	5.3		4.4	4.3	3.8	3.4	B
Mexico				2.8	2.6	2.6	2.1	C
Morocco	5.1	6.4	7.6	7.9				
Nicaragua	2.4	3.2	4.0		6.3			B
Pakistan	2.2	1.8	1.9	1.9	2.0	2.1		B
Panama	5.7	5.0		5.2	5.2	5.2	5.0	C
Paraguay[2]	1.6	1.6	2.2	2.0	1.6	1.5		B
Peru	3.4	3.1		2.9	2.9	2.9		C
Philippines	1.9	1.6		1.8	1.3	1.3	1.7	C
Rwanda	2.3	2.7		3.3	3.3			A
Sri Lanka	2.8	3.1		3.0	2.8	3.0	3.5	B
Swaziland[2]	3.7	5.6	5.3				5.8	A
Syrian Arab Republic[1]	3.9	4.5		6.2	6.2	6.4	6.6	B

Country	1975	1980	1982	1983	1984	1985	1986	Group
United Republic of Tanzania[1]		5.1	4.3	4.0	4.0	4.3		
Thailand	3.6	3.3	3.9	3.9	3.9	3.9		C
Togo	3.5	5.6		6.2	6.2	5.4	5.2	A
Trinidad and Tobago		3.0	3.7	5.6	5.9	6.0	5.9	C
Tunisia	5.2	5.4	5.5		5.9	5.9		B
Turkey		2.8		3.4	2.6	2.3	2.1	C
United Arab Emirates	1.0	1.4		1.8	1.8	1.9	2.3	B
Uruguay		2.2			2.4	2.6	3.1	C
Venezuela[6]	5.3	5.2	6.7	8.1	6.1	6.8		C
Zambia	6.7		5.5	5.7	5.4			A
Zimbabwe	3.6	6.6	7.2	7.6	7.7			A

1. Including operating and capital expenditure 1980–86 (Bahrain), 1984 (Chile), 1985 (Colombia), 1986 (Dominican Republic), 1980–85 (Iraq and Bengladesh), 1975–86 (Syrian Arab Republic), 1984 and 1985 (United Republic of Tanzania).
2. Ministry of Education only in 1980 to 1985 (Bengladesh), 1975 to 1986 (Colombia), 1980 to 1986 (Dominican Republic), 1975 and 1980 (Japan and Kenya), 1975 (Swaziland).
3. Including intermediate colleges in 1980 to 1984 (Bengladesh).
4. Public subsidies to private education excluded in 1975 and 1980 (Japan).
5. Scholarships and allocations for studies abroad included in 1980 and 1985 (Mali).
6. Central government expenditures only in 1984 and 1985 (India) and 1980 to 1984 (Venezuela).

Source: UNESCO, *Statistical Yearbook 1988*, Table 4.3.

TABLE A14. Percentage of GNP devoted to third–level education (ranking of a few countries, 1980 and 1985)

Country	Rank 1980	Rank 1985	Group
Botswana	4	2	A
Kenya	6	6	A
Zimbabwe	7	1	A
Togo	11	12	A
Madagascar	13	28	A
Mali	23	28	A
Honduras	26	17	A
Malawi	26	30	A
Cameroon	29	22	A

TABLE A14 – *continued*

Country	Rank 1980	Rank 1985	Group
Burkina Faso	36	35	A
Bangladesh	44	41	A
Costa Rica	1	16	B
Jordan	8	3	B
Malaysia	9	7	B
Tunisia	13	10	B
Mauritius	15	22	B
Syrian Arab Republic	20	8	B
Sri Lanka	30	32	B
Gabon	33	18	B
Bahrain	33	22	B
Iraq	36	22	B
China	38	35	B
Colombia	40	33	B
Pakistan	41	40	B
Paraguay	42	42	B
Cuba	3	9	C
Ecuador	11	26	C
Venezuela	16	5	C
Panama	18	13	C
Chile	19	18	C
Trinidad and Tobago	21	10	C
Korea (Republic of)	21	15	C
Argentina	23	39	C
Brazil	25	30	C
Thailand	26	21	C
Peru	30	33	C
India	32	26	C
Turkey	33	38	C
Uruguay	39	37	C
Philippines	42	43	C
Canada	2	4	D
Japan	10	14	D

Notes: see Table A13.

Source: UNESCO, *Statistical Yearbook 1988,* Table 4.3.

TABLE A15. Urban population in developing regions

Region	1980 (millions)	1980 (%)	2000 (%)
Latin America	359.5	64.8	84.0[1]
Africa	133.0	28.9	42.5
East Asia	359.5	33.1	45.4
Southern Asia	329.8	23.1	34.9

1. In 2025

Source: J. Hardoy et al., *Conversaciones sobre la ciudad del Tercer Mundo*, Buenos Aires, Grupo Editor Latinoamericanos, 1989.

TABLE A16. Urban population in cities of over 4 million

Region	Year	%
Latin America	2025	30.0
Africa	2025	34.0
East Asia	2000	9.1
Southern Asia	2000	8.4

Source: J. Hardoy et al., *Conversaciones sobre la ciudad del Tercer Mundo*, Buenos Aires, Grupo Editor Latinoamericanos, 1989.

TABLE A17. Urban population in substandard conditions, 1980

City	%
Kinshasa	60
Calcutta	65
Mexico	46
Lima	70
La Paz	64
Calcutta	37
Delhi	65
Luanda	70
Maputo	80
Addis Ababa	79
Nairobi	40
São Paulo	55
Santiago de Chile	25
Buenos Aires	30
Guayaquil	70
Lima	40
Bogotá	59

Source: J. Hardoy et al., *Conversaciones sobre la ciudad del Tercer Mundo,* Buenos Aires, Grupo Editor Latinoamericanos, 1989.